BEYOND TH ⎯⎯⎯⎯

'This delightful books tells of youth, vigour and innocence pitted against penury, misfortune and a hostile climate' *Fife Free Press*

'Richard Frere is a fine writer and his account of his joys and sorrows is immensely readable'
Aberdeen Advertiser

'I enjoyed every word . . . Richard Frere is totally honest, and he's a good, graphic writer'
Chronicle Midweek, Reading

Richard Frere

Beyond
The Highland Line

CORGI BOOKS

BEYOND THE HIGHLAND LINE

A CORGI BOOK 0 552 12501 6

Originally published in Great Britain
by John Murray (Publishers) Ltd.

PRINTING HISTORY
John Murray edition published 1984
Corgi edition published 1985

Corgi Books are published by Transworld Publishers Ltd.,
Century House, 61-63 Uxbridge Road, Ealing, London W5 5SA,
in Australia by Transworld Publishers (Aust.) Pty. Ltd.,
26 Harley Crescent, Condell Park, NSW 2200, and in New
Zealand by Transworld Publishers (N.Z.) Ltd., Cnr. Moselle
and Waipareira Avenues, Henderson, Auckland.

Made and printed in Great Britain by
Hunt Barnard Printing Ltd., Aylesbury, Bucks.

Contents

To the dauntless heroine of the story,
my dear wife, Joan

1 ❦ *Third Class Single*

'Well, there it is!' I said and added in an undertone: 'It's ours.'

Joan, my young wife, gave me a complex look. It sprang from shock, surprise, and dawning comprehension: it hinted that she had not been without her suspicions before and stated very clearly that she was outraged to find them justified now.

'You haven't bought *that*, surely?' She knew full well that I had. I was cornered so I became truculent: 'Yes, what else could I have done? Where can you find a house for five hundred pounds? You know we've looked and looked. Besides, it's got possibilities, surely you can see that.'

'Nonsense! It's not a *house*.' Her fury knew no bounds. 'Who could live here in the winter? It's dreadful. We could never do anything with it. And what a depressing place this is!'

The bone of our contention stood unashamedly on top of a small grassy mound not far away. As a dwelling it was (as I know now) grotesque, but in retrospect it is hard to recapture a state of mind.

'Anyway, let's go and have a look round', I invited, and led the way up a grassy path which ended at a door. Proudly I took a key from my pocket. 'It isn't as bad as you think', I claimed as I stuck the key in a rusty lock. She followed in a cold fury.

The Sun Bungalow, Station Road, Carr Bridge, Inverness-shire, was certainly unusual. It consisted of three obsolete carriages of the old Highland Railway which, in the late evening of their lives, had ended up on top of a hillock of sand and had subsequently been arranged in the form of a rough H. Two passenger coaches had been set parallel to each other and were joined like Siamese twins by a guardsvan. The first owners had added to this simple design by making use of the carriage walls as support for three roofs of corrugated iron. The new rooms thus created were a lightly built glass-fronted chamber – described in the scanty sales literature as a 'sun lounge'; a gloomy, cavernous department, as dark as the other was bright, ill-lit by three small skylights; and a much more robust and homely room designed as a kitchen. This was fitted with a monstrous black range, a chipped sink and a copper boiler heated from the range. It had two fixed plate-glass windows and its floor was composed of railway sleepers.

We walked round slowly, saying nothing. Although it was only early Autumn the evening air held a touch of frost. The bungalow stood at nearly the highest part of the village and cold air had begun to cascade down from the yet higher moorland ridges round about. But in the 'sun lounge' the heat still lingered; the glass frames made no concession to ventilation and a stale necrotic smell rose from the dead flies which lay in ranks on the long window sill. At the far end of the room was a small fireplace with glazed tiles. It was stuffed with yellow newspapers and ancient ashes. 'Oh God, no!' muttered Joan, her love of the sturdily medieval grossly affronted by this late Victorian niceness.

Since the coaches had no corridors, each compartment had to be entered by its own door. All the windows had leather straps. There were notices warning passengers not to put their heads through the windows for fear of sparks. A lavatory had been fitted into one of the compartments, alongside a small bath, but I looked in vain for the prohibition which in these new circumstances must have advocated eternal constipation.

While all these things fascinated me Joan was strongly unimpressed. She remained darkly quiet, slowly filling up with revulsion. She responded in no way to my vision when I spoke desperately of what might be done to make it splendid. 'No one could make it splendid. There's nothing here to build on. I only wanted a solid, old house. In England!' This matter of where we should live had always been a point of issue between us. Her home had been in

Sussex. She was also six months pregnant and we had no money. But still I went on muttering: 'We had no choice.' This was only true, as I see it now, because I had allowed my choice to erode away, and was determined to stay in the wild Highlands against all the odds.

Suddenly there was a mighty rumble: an express train went roaring by, quite out of breath. The railway line was about two hundred yards away. The bungalow trembled slightly and a few flies were shaken on to the floor. Gradually the windows stopped rattling. Oddly enough, despite its powerful violence it was a friendly sound and in all the nights that made up the years we were to spend there, or in all the days, it never gave offence.

My wife wanted fresh air. We went outside. The evening was beautiful and tended to embellish the rather indifferent prospect. The best part of it was the forest that bounded our ground to the east: its floor was thick with mats of pine needles and clumps of juniper and heather. That was at the back of the house. To the front our view was of the Station Road, a group of railway cottages, a signal box, some sheds and to the left the outline of the station itself.

Our own ground extended to one-fifth of an acre, was infertile and possibly impermanent. The person who had sold me the bungalow had been reticent when asked about the titles to the land. Now it seemed that the land belonged to British Railways who for personal reasons reserved the right to require us to remove the buildings, etc. from it on being given twenty-one days notice. Even to me this gave a certain sense of insecurity though I had, in those days, very little tendency to anxiety over important things. Joan, I think, probably regarded it as an escape clause in a contract which had been forced upon her.

Because it was laid upon a glacial moraine, the soil grew poor grass and what there was looked like a well-worn cheap carpet. A few broom shrubs made flashes of yellow gold in odd corners of our patch while, on the bank on which the buildings stood, a few birch trees had a browned-off Autumn look. Below the bank was a wooden garage. It was better built than the house. Leaning against its open door and still sweating oil from a fast run was our transport, a well-used BSA motor cycle whose mechanical health had absorbed my loving attention for the past year. Its demands, and those of my mountains, had left me, during that time, insufficient daylight to attend to anything else.

Our local situation may have been suburban but the country outside it was pure magic to me. The station road is a short cul-de-sac: it leaves the road up the Dulnain valley and ends a few hundred yards on at the station. The valley road climbs easily beside the river until it reaches the high farm of Dalnahaitnach. Here it turns towards the north and eventually rejoins the main Inverness to Perth road near the Slochd summit, a high, windswept spot where road and railway are crushed together in a narrow gap. The country-side round here is ancient, primal moorland studded with high-set lochs with shores of sand and pebble and low escarpments of clean grey rock. Overhead the buzzards hang, mewing to each other or intent with staring eyes, and in the thick springy heather the chicks of the grouse run in season. The roots of the heather are deeply planted in the acid peat: in the peat jutting eerily or lying flat like old bones, are the bleached reminders of the ancient, vanished forests. Long, dark and winding, the peaty corridors quarter the land carrying the slow water down to the larger streams: from these to the rivers, mostly to the twisting, unhurried Dulnain who in turn adds his quota of brown flood to that of his famous brother, the Spey.

Below the moors it is a country of forests. Scots pine abound, large or small, in military ranks or as proud and venerable people of the woods, and here too is the grace of the faery birch. In winter the keen harp of the north wind will twang and whistle in the roofless garrets of the forests while the snow piles high and deep behind banks and pulls down branches to the ground. After the blizzard comes the frost, an ocean of cold in this high land that fixes it in a white silence. Gradually, grudgingly winter finally yields to a brief uncertain Spring, the trees get dressed and decent and the rivers, swollen with melted snow, run loud and hearty. But deception is the mood of this Spring, a loose lady who flirts with both sun and snow, for no sooner is there a promise of warm days than a blustering bustle of hail storms in across the hills and all turns white again. It is the lambing storm, hard on humans and little lambs alike.

If Spring is a flirt, summer is a cautious mistress. It touches and it does not touch. Here is the mood and country of Maurice Walsh. Below the craggy Dulsie Bridge, in the wide plain around Lochindorb, his simple heroes poached and strode and fought, like gusts of fresh morning air, when bold men, back from the First War, were surprised to be alive and girls still had regard for their maidenheads.

This far east the summer sun is not without warmth and often the plateau heats up like an oven top and the pavements of peat will support a man, though cracked like crazy paving. In the forest the stolid pines get hot and bothered and sweat red resin or stand mute to the thunder as it walks heavy booted down the sky.

The autumn comes in a haze of white frosted mornings and golden blue days. The paper-thin leaves drift down the windless air and mock the rainbow with their colours. The hills, dusted with snow, stand clear, returned to perfect focus, spiced with the scent of fading heather and rusting bracken. It is truly beautiful, the year's justification and its reward.

But out local situation was still suburban, and my point of view under strong siege. We continued to look around our new domain but nothing therein pleased my wife. She had crowned herself with discontent and would not abdicate her throne. I searched desperately for anything that might bring her even the smallest spark of hope, but it was a task for the faithful. A dead rat, lying conspicuously in our path, did nothing to improve matters. Its symbolism made her wince and I took its presence as a personal attack, a thing designed to promote discord. When she had passed by with averted eyes I kicked the thing and it squelched into shapelessness. I saw that it was heartily beset by maggots.

The fence that encircled our property was dead of metal fatigue and dry rot. At some time the grass had been burnt and many of the post bottoms were burnt away like charred matchsticks. Rabbit tracks depressed the ground from the direction of the pines and formed truculent little roads: it was clear that their makers came and went as though by right immemorial. It did not matter. There was nothing to eat here, nothing at least that we could share.

I became aware that my advocacy, for want of anything to fire it, was beginning to go out. Yet Joan seemed suddenly to have found something to interest her. She was looking at the bank below the house. I hastened hopefully to her side. Our separate moods are like the globes of an hour glass: as one fills up the other drains away. We are seldom perfectly happy at the same time but neither are we met in the lowest moments. 'We could have a rockery here – I suppose', she suggested in a voice carefully devoid of intention, just in case I might use it in evidence later. 'It might be nice here, just below the birch tree.' She prodded the ground with a stick: at once some broken bottles grated and a few rusty tins came to light. The sheer sordidness of it killed her little mood. She cried out: 'I hate it here. I want to leave this horrible place!'

But it was to be five years before her wish came true.

Our son Richard Tudor was born in late November in the nearby village of Grantown on Spey. Our daughter Heather was then two years old. Such tender flowers would have been blasted black by the intense cold in the unconverted bungalow, and it was a cold year even by the chilly standards of the Dulnain Valley. It was our great good fortune that in searching for temporary accommodation in Carr Bridge we had met Jim and Shiela Wilshin who ran a guest house on the south road. The Wilshins were not professional hoteliers; they were people of taste and formerly of substance who treated their customers as they would their friends. Sympathetic to our predicament they took us in and their friendship was as valuable to us as the immaculate hospitality of their house. My plan was to do what I could as quickly as possible to make the bungalow habitable: until I achieved this my wife had too much concern for her children to move in. Speed was of the essence, our means were too slender to permit a protracted stay at Struan House, and I saw March of the new year as the absolute deadline.

I brought Joan and our very new son from the hospital in Grantown, collected Heather from the possessive care of my mother, who lived in Inverness, and settled them comfortably with the Wilshins. I stayed one night with my family and vowed it would be the last until I had put my house in order. Struan House was everything that the bungalow was not: it would have been easy to have succumbed to its warmth and comfort.

So I began to put my untried building skills to the test. Fortunately I am blessed with dexterity and the ability to put my hands to new uses but at this time I was pitifully uninformed and inexperienced. I could hit a nail on the head, bore a hole with a brace and bit, hold a sharp saw along a pencil line on wood, and cement two bricks together. That was it.

The bungalow's limitations as a winter home now became painfully clear. As such it had never been intended. In fact the former owner had told me that he only let it to summer visitors. In those days, of course, there *were* no winter visitors: the great Cairngorm sports bonanza was still some years away. For five months in every year our new home, along with many other more substantial dwellings in the area, was allowed to hibernate. When I first came in early December the water supply was frozen solid and had been, I suspected, for some weeks. Apart from the lack of water for domestic purposes it made heating difficult. There were only two places where a fire might be lit. The small tiled fireplace in the 'sun lounge' – a name now scrapped in favour of the more seemly 'sitting room' – was one of these but although I managed to get hold of some coal and made a cheery blaze, the heat from the tiny hearth was lost in the big room with its wide area of glass and slight construction. The old range in the kitchen seemed to offer more hope: a permanent warmth in that room would provide a little oasis of comfort in this very bleak house. It was not to be, for ice filled all the copper veins of the system and to light more than a token fire would be to run the risk of explosion.

As you read these pages you may notice that I am fated to commit self-destructive acts. About three weeks after my entry I did, in fact, kindle too big a fire which burst the boiler in the cooker. It blew off the fire door and filled the kitchen with steam and flaming ashes.

It was a white Christmas and Boxing Day was whiter still. The pines bowed low to the Snow King and a voracious frost bit the edges off the short days. The path which I used on my brief daily visits to Struan was a white-walled corridor through which no sound escaped. I gave up my work to spend two days of Christmas with my family. We enjoyed the time together. Joan's spirits had risen. She was glad to be rid of the incumbent in her womb and delighted, as I suspect most mothers are, to find it perfectly equipped with head, arms, legs, fingers and toes all in their right places and in the proper numbers. She still viewed the prospect of living in the Bungalow with distaste but anger had taken the place of distress and I knew that, being a young woman of great determination, she would fully accept the challenge and make a life for us there as soon as I had satisfied the conditions for her entry.

I went back to the Bungalow. My brief sojourn amid the fleshpots had unnerved me for my return to this sordid Sparta. It was desperately miserable. The temperature was constantly below freezing inside the building and the absence of water made a mockery of domestic hygiene. I am the kind of man who seems to attract muddle and in three weeks of my occupation a shocking mess had accrued. Unable to wash up plates, I had piled dirty ones upon each other until an accordion of china mounted from the floor, its segments joined together by grease and frost. During my short absence my hot water bottle – a psychological no less than a physical necessity – had frozen solid in my bed and it took me hours to thaw the contents in its rubber bladder.

I dithered, dabbling at this and that. I was quite without system. I knew that my first task was to remove all the compartments from one carriage which would be redivided into two rooms and a small hall, the latter designed to act as a den and passage between the sitting room and the rest of the house. This is what Joan, who was the architect, intended: but Joan was not there. Her visits were deliberately infrequent. She had told me firmly that she would stay at Struan House until certain things were done at the Bungalow and from this nothing would make her budge.

Bored and discouraged by interminable demolition, I put aside my wrecking bar and began to paint the sitting room door. I felt it necessary to have a glimpse of the final glory, but the brief deviation proved unwise. I found I was no painter and to paint in those days required skill. In the evening it looked beautiful but by morning! I had applied it too thickly and in the early light the paint hung down in folds and creases. I prayed that critical Joan would not choose this moment for an unscheduled visit, though in fact it might have done much good, for her single-mindedness was what was needed.

In fact the gutting-out of the carriages only took about ten days although it seemed much longer. At length all the leather and wooden entrails lay outside in the snow and I sat on a box and looked down the full stretch of the coach. It was roughly done and splintered in places, but it was clear, a clean sweep. Now, I thought, the real fun will begin.

It began.

From the village joiner I bought a quantity of planking and three steel-framed windows. The joiner, Jim McKendry, was a cheerful man with a glowing red face fringed all round with white stubble. Most carpenters are like this, I have found; a breed apart, happy and helpful. Without delay he brought my materials up to the Bungalow in his trailer and gave me as much advice as I asked for. He told me, for instance, that saws *can* be sharpened, a point upon which I had been ignorant. As a boy I had led a sheltered life. My last saw had dulled its gleaming youth on hard mahogany and brass screws: it had neither set nor any cutting edges and jammed tightly in the first few inches of a cut. I had thrown it away in the belief that its sickness was inoperable.

Joan made one of her visits. She looked well and pretty, and I would have liked her to stay with me. But she only came to give her opinion as to where the new windows should be fitted. We decided that two of them should open onto the forest while the third should be so positioned as to catch the setting sun behind the signal box. When I had walked her back to Struan and returned to my celibate existence I worked out my frustrations by hacking out the holes for the windows from the ribs of the coach.

Soon the window frames were in place. From outside the whole thing looked very ramshackle. The rigid steel frames mated badly with the tough hardwood structure of the coach, much of which had been chopped and split in order to make a large-enough opening. Lumps of wood and even folded cardboard had been employed to fill the gaps while the frames were secured in place by a mixture of nails and screws. I had, however, managed to obtain a uniform level – as measured from the running board of the coach – and the frames were flush with the inside surfaces. The job which followed, the lining of the inside walls, brought me great satisfaction. The cutting and fitting of the clean, white, slotted wood, was fine and precise: it was a therapy after my rough butchery of the carcase of the coach. With quantities of sandpaper and a big plane to come to my rescue when eye and rule were found in error, I pressed on fanatically until the job was done. How well it looked! I swept up all the bits and threw them out of the windows, the better to savour it. And how grand the fresh new resinous timber smelt: it took away the frowst of the old carriages and competed with the sour cooking odours which my domestic incompetency had produced.

My first thought was that my wife must see it. But before that I would paint it. I went to Grantown on the early bus and came back with a large pot of varnish. It was a dark brown stain. What prompted me to make this sober choice is a mystery to me now. It was perhaps connected with a basic gloom in my nature. At any rate as soon as I was done I realised that this was a bad thing. Joan, with the normal live person's aversion to coffins, would not be inspired.

Not only did it look like a coffin, the room was as cold as death. To glaze the windows was a first priority. I consulted McKendry who with his usual helpfulness offered to supply the pieces of glass cut to size. I would have none of it. Puffed out with pride in my stubborn intention to try all things for myself I ordered the glass in sheets. It came, safely crated. Mad with impatience I slid out a sheet, laid it upon a rough surface and drew my new tool across it in the way I had seen it done. There was a sharp crack and the thing exploded. The casual stroke, the easy off-hand snap, were not, somehow, for me. Wastage was well over the odds and the puttying a boring chore, but finally all the panes were in place.

I was pleased with my air-tight room but the more I saw of my dark brown walls the more I regretted them. I tried to forget about this. Joan who had formerly shown such a cautious interest in her new home now became suspicious because I had not asked her to applaud my latest efforts. I felt that I must present her with something new and surprising to offset my choice of decoration and decided to install a wash basin.

With my continuing mania for acquiring new tools which I had not the skill to use I had obtained plumber's 'drifts' and springs and a fine hack-saw. Before long a length of pipe protruded from the hot cylinder in the kitchen and made its ostentatious way to the bedroom where it ended abruptly in a tap. When we had hot water it would obviously work, but the waste flow posed a new problem. The earth pipe was twenty feet away concealed in rock-hard frozen ground and I hadn't the slightest idea how to effect a joint. I resorted to the primitive principle of 'gardez loo', bored a hole in the carriage floor and inserted a short waste pipe. Soapy water is inoffensive and would surely take care of itself, I thought.

I summoned Joan and she came. The exterior of the coach with its shoddy incongruities was so obviously only in a transient state that she dismissed it with: 'We'll have to have a wall round here,' and went inside. She has always had a 'genie with the lamp' attitude to ways and means which leaves me a little breathless. She graciously approved the clean sweep of the new room and smiled indulgently at the Heath Robinson washbasin. She seemed bewildered by the varnish. 'Will it come off?' she enquired sweetly and then hardened: 'You do realise that I wouldn't sleep in this room with that filthy brown stuff on the walls, don't you?'

I regarded my misguided taste bitterly, realising that I had probably postponed cohabitation for a very long time.

As will have been gathered we were poor, but our poverty was not the kind which leads to desperation. I had been brought up in a home where money, being sufficient, was not mentioned as a daily factor in one's thinking. So had Joan. But now things had changed. My father, who had died in the last year of the war, had indulged my passion for the outdoor life to the exclusion of a practical training for a profession and with his death the means which made him independent were much reduced, though they still added up to a substantial estate. He left my mother the life interest and she, a kindly yet madly possessive person, meted out money to us, or rather to me, on the unspoken understanding that I should always be available at her call. Every so often my eroded manhood resisted this subject state and I would make feeble attempts to find work.

This was one of these times. Joan's refusal to take up married life in a refrigerator meant a continued drain on my grace and favour resources. Jim Wilshin's hotel bills, modest though they were, had to be met, the more so because they were so modest, and a sense of urgency settled on me like a dark cloud. I went out to find a job.

It was not hard to find. The local industry was forestry, then gradually becoming less dominant after the massive fellings of the recent war, but there were still large mills in the area. One of these, not more than a mile from our door, required a time keeper. It occurred to me that even one totally unversed in the ways of industry should be able to pick up a thing like that. I telephoned the manager, a Mr McMaster, and asked for an appointment.

McMaster was large and florid. He greeted me with a powerful handshake which I returned with equal pressure. 'Ex officer?' he asked. I made no comment on this for I saw no reason to disabuse his mind of so flattering assessment of my wartime performance. In fact I had risen no higher than full corporal, good character being allowed in view of crimes undetected.

'Sit down, then', ordered McMaster, and I subsided uneasily. He continued: 'Done anything like this before? Last job?'

'No, nothing like this. And well, last job –' I broke off: the idle days stood up in a row, rebuking me. 'No job at all since the war', I concluded.

It didn't seem to worry him. 'Not to worry. You'll be responsible for seeing the bods turn up at seven o'clock. Watch them closely. They're a lot of damn liberty takers. But none of your military discipline here – mark that, my lad. These chaps can come and go, and there's plenty of timber work around. Finish at five, unless there's overtime. We'd pay you four pounds a week, is that enough?' I was hardly in a position to bargain but I did have the effrontery to suggest that a further five shillings might be added to allow me to run my motor-cycle on the job. McMaster, surprisingly, seemed to like the idea.

It began by working out well. My duties between seven a.m. and five p.m. were quite nebulous – except on Fridays when I helped to measure the timber stock in the yards – and I found that as long as I kept out of sight nothing was asked of me. So between these times I went back to the

Bungalow and I was able to do a lot of work. My first job there was to remedy the brown stain in the bedroom and substitute the colour of my wife's choice. I distempered it hopefully but it only lasted for three days in its pristine beauty. After that it cracked and flaked as the water paint dried out. I lined the walls with plasterboard, which I had just discovered, cutting the amenable material with a dressmaker's care, and nailed it on top of the wood. It was an extravagance inspired by my sudden earning capacity but it was to prove a godsend: it was a joy to paint, looked smooth and neat but above all it added insulation. I knew it would please Joan and, filled with growing confidence, I went to Jim McKendry for two doors and wood for framing the partitions. I laboured fanatically for two nights and days. All at once I was finished; there were two nice little rooms and the tiny hall cum den between them.

The snow-filled golden days and the bitter nights extended well into March without a break. But a change was in the air. As I walked down to Struan to persuade my wife to join me in our new home, a grey stain was thickening in the west. Before it ran a small, soft, freshening wind. Yesterday's fluffy snow now crunched beneath my feet and from the overburdened pines a slow drip-drip of water made pock marks in the white carpet. All around the world it seemed that winter's long grip was relaxing like a tired hand. It struck me as a timely omen.

Joan was satisfied. She had keyed herself up to accept what must still be a marathon task. It was a brave decision for the Bungalow was not what she wanted nor where she wanted to be. Apart from the bedrooms the rest of the house had gained in squalor. Planks and building materials lay about everywhere, a clutch of nails sat in the congealed fat of a frying pan, cement had been mixed and allowed to set in a domestic mixing bowl.

We sat, smoking cigarettes, a little uneasy of each other in this new wooing. The thaw had found a counterpart in Joan's heart, but it took a bizarre event to spark off her final acquiescence. A loud crash sounded from the kitchen. My pile of plates, their frosty bond broken at last, had tumbled to the floor and all had been demolished. Joan, looking businesslike, put out her cigarette: 'It's high time I was here', she said with savage resignation, 'this nonsense can't go on!'

So our life together at the Bungalow, in the Station Road of the village of Carr Bridge, began. We had no hot water, no electricity, no telephone, only a primus to cook on, two Tilley lamps, and two very young children, But we had our youth and a joint determination to survive, and these are warrior qualities which have the power to scatter an army of misfortunes.

Added to which, of course, I had my mountains.

2 ❋ Child's play

Staring down the years that nowadays vault over each other's backs with increasingly indecent haste, I discern that our first few months at the Bungalow were the best we were to have there. The challenge might have been an indifferent one but we were fresh to it. Joan's presence proved a spur to my intent and lent it a firm direction. I dithered less and when I took up my tools I found an increasing rapport with them.

Spring came almost overnight in a flood of tepid rain and the Dulnain River writhed and shouldered its way beneath the thin arch of the Coffin Bridge at the end of our road. The children settled in. Richard lay in his pram in the clear, strong sunlight, sleeping, kicking or gurgling as the mood took him while Heather wore out more than one pair of small shoes braking her tricycle on the steep little slopes of our moraine. There was a sense of morning in our moods. It was, as remembered nostalgically, rather good; and though nostalgia is a great liar, or a camera with a faulty filter, it couldn't have been that bad.

My mother had recognised my entry into the profession of time-keeping by giving us a small lump sum. It is only true to say that I had described my job to her in much grander terms than it merited and I also implied that it had prospects, which was a downright lie. The only prospects were dismissal or lifelong acceptance of a completely dead-end occupation. Time-keepers in saw mills are not subject to advancement.

With the money we bought a Rayburn cooker and had the house wired for electricity. Joan put away the primus stove on which she had grown used to performing miracles. In theory the kitchen could now be heated, and so could the water, had we had any. Unfortunately when frost unlocked its grip on our water works only the original tiny trickle returned. It gradually filled up the cistern so that we could light the Rayburn safely but it took many minutes to fill a kettle and a bath had to be planned twenty-four hours in advance. For once I felt unequal to going it alone. I found a local plumber and invited his opinion.

The plumber was a taciturn man. He carried out his examination and used his apparatus in an atmosphere of gloom and despair. The thing he brought looked like a stirrup pump. He attached it to a tap and pumped air into the system for five minutes. When he removed it a gush of dirty water and some drowned worms spewed into the sink. Then it stopped completely, even the trickle had ceased.

Wordless, he prepared to leave. 'Aren't you going to try something else?' demanded Joan crossly. He gave her a glum look. 'Canna dae onything', he stated flatly, 'yon's a block at the mains. Pumping just made it worse.'

'Can't you dig it up?' I asked reasonably.

'Nae, I canna do that. A' wraxed me back twa year ago.'

'Well', I said, 'I'll just have to do it myself. Will you tell me where I ought to dig?'

I followed him down to the Station Road. 'It's doon there.' He indicated an invisible point beneath the hard tarmac. 'You'll hae to get permission from the Roads to dig.'

I took the news to my wife. We decided that I should do the work that Sunday. People drove up the road to meet trains on Saturday and every other day I was time-keeping. I approached the Department of Roads. My problem was not, it seemed, unique, and they had become accustomed to being helpful. They offered me a red lantern in case the work went on after dark. I devoutly hoped that I shouldn't need it.

At first light on that Sabbath morning I judged the spot and began to crack asphalt. It was very hard work. Below the crust was hard packed gravel. As I gradually sank below the surface I became obsessed with the thought that I was probably in quite the wrong place. Soon a large mound of gravel occupied the centre of the road. As morning advanced a few pious church-goers stole by with carefully averted faces, not a Samaritan among them. A single car carefully edged its way around my excavation. At six feet I struck hard pan which had the look of having been untroubled since the world began. I knew then that I must have missed the pipe.

With growing desperation I tunnelled in all directions. Nothing, except the final closure of the road to motor vehicles, came of it. The short spring day was running its course. Two cars came down the road and after brief inspections went back the way they had come. It was plain that I was becoming a public nuisance but to abandon the thing at this stage was unthinkable. I lit my red lantern and placed it firmly on top of the mound of gravel.

Back underground, a torch gripped in my teeth, I had given up my spade and was using my hands. Suddenly I felt a smooth round surface in the midst of sticky clay and gravel. My heart bounded! Success, and then more success! A few feet away here was our own pipe and the junction with the main. Emotionally I scrambled out and rushed up to the Bungalow to tell Joan about it. A dramatic factor in my personality demands a preparation of the stage.

I hooked a large spanner round the nut which screwed our pipe to the Waterboard's. It moved easily and was free in seconds. A monstrous gush of water followed it out. I would not have exchanged my state with that of kings. In the sheer delight of success I allowed valuable time to slip away while the rushing water bored into the side of the hole and brought down a landslide of silt and gravel. Big boulders were loosened and fell heavily into the pit. Hastily I grabbed the pipe and shoved it into the other. It was like a drunk man trying to make love. The water was up to my elbows, it poured into my boots, on every side the walls of the pit were collapsing. There was a slithering sound and a huge weight settled against my leg, pinning it against the main pipe. I struggled to release my foot from the boulder but to no avail. Another fell just behind my knee forcing me into a position of servile genuflection.

As I fiddled with the joint it came to me rather bleakly that I could possibly be drowned. Though I struggled desperately I could not move and the water was up to my chest while the lower part of me was buried in heavy unyielding sludge. It was utterly bizarre but so were many cases one read about in which people lost their lives in domestic accidents. In my mind's eye I could clearly read an obituary beginning: 'Suddenly, in unusual circumstances . . .' and thus stimulated I put all my strength into one tremendous tug. It worked, my leg came free and I was able to stand up. Prudence prompted me to scramble to safety but a stubborn anger kept me where I was. I took a deep breath and pushed my head under the water.

This time my boldness was rewarded. It isn't often. Once again, by some miracle, I found both pipes, and by a greater one managed to slot the male into the female. Copulation was achieved. I came up for breath then dived again to screw the nut up tight.

At the Bungalow Joan was truly delighted. When I had squelched through the door she gave me a look of respect. On the Rayburn a kettle boiled briskly and throughout the house the pipes were singing for pure joy.

It was a year of incidents, good, bad and simply ridiculous. I often thought of Judge Brack's astounded remark in *Hedda Gabler*: 'People just don't do these things', and wondered why I always proved an exception. The loss of some of our heirlooms was one example. I had recently bought some thick planks from the sawmill to build some kitchen shelves. When they were set in position they made a handsome show, thick, white and solid. The floor of uneven railway sleepers suffered badly by comparison. So we had a plan to improve that too by covering it with a layer of concrete deep enough to make a level surface.

To find room to work I had to remove the legs which supported the shelves. They were fixed to the walls behind; in front I supported them by wedges. It was a custom of our partnership that after Joan had made her design I would carry out the work privily. I am a frantic exhibitionist but only in spheres in which I consider myself completely competent.

Throughout the centuries our families had hoarded silver. Some of it had come our way. A number of items, exquisitely polished, had been set out on the shelves. It didn't occur to me that under the circumstances it might have made good sense to remove them out of harm's way. By late evening I had a deep bed of fast-setting concrete extending half way across the room. I curbed Joan's curiosity and told her that I would not let her see my splendid work until the morning.

It was a night of wind. The house banged and shook. It banged and shook so loudly that we didn't hear the shelves fall down. Inevitably morning came.

Very proudly I said: 'Well, what do you think of that, darling?' and flung the door wide. Joan, seldom at a loss for words, was speechless. So was I. The edges of the shelves were half buried in a rigid grey mass and of the silver there was hardly any sign at all. A set of Georgian teaspoons had settled out of sight. A nineteenth-century sauce boat could be seen only as a blurred outline in the concrete. Knives, forks, casters, snuff boxes and an entire inkstand were entombed without trace. Only the lip of an entrée dish and the handle of a silver teapot stood proud of the surface, the latter's shape pointedly suggesting a question mark. I could not bear its symbolism and gave it a firm tug. It broke off, glad, I imagined, to be free.

The cement had been mixed to set quickly. It was as hard as a rock. We tried to recover only the entrée dish but the chisel I used inflicted much damage. Joan who loves old and beautiful things was nearly in tears. I was unhappy in my guilt: the floor, otherwise quite successful, was always to have a slight stigma attached. Later when the first shock had faded we wondered how future generations of archaeologists might interpret such a find. Would they seek a mummified body, believing this to have been an act of some late subscriber to the pharaonic custom by which no man of station went empty-handed on his way?

Some incidents were simply ridiculous. Many of them concerned by 1931 BSA motorcycle which I had bought from an RAF mechanic for five pounds. A late starter in most things, I was twenty-six years old before I discovered motorcycles but when I did, the sport became an obsession with me. In the year of disgrace following my demob when I might have been better occupied in planning a career, my whole attention had been fixed upon the riding and tuning of this modest machine and the ease with which it would take me into the mountains. Joan, at some personal risk, would often sit upon my pillion: sometimes she was asked to perform duties well beyond the scope of the average passenger. Once as we crossed the snow-bound Lechd summit, both the clutch and accelerator cables broke simultaneously and I handed her two pieces of wire which she was to pull or release in order to control the speed of the machine. On another occasion, bound for Grantown, the BSA caught fire. A spark from the ignition set off petrol from a leaking pipe. We were just on the outskirts of the town when I shouted 'Jump for it!' as a fan of flame burst out from beneath the tank. Joan, always prepared for the abnormal, vaulted clear and landed upright from a speed of twenty miles an hour. It was fortunate that she had an early familiarity with the horse. Very hot about the crotch and fearful lest my oily trousers should catch fire I swerved into an opening between two houses where kindly Fate had provided a heap of sand. Soon the fire was out: the sturdy machine was none the worse.

Joan was not with me to share the incident of the coat. The coat concerned was a vastly unbecoming part of my wardrobe, yet a practical one. Since I have never had a sophisticated taste in dress I rather fancied myself in this great leather thing which had once been the property of a Russian officer. Had it been a good fit it would have been suited perfectly for its new role, but it was far too long in the skirts. Anyone but I could see that sooner or later it would get wound up in my chain.

When the inevitable happened I was again in Grantown, drawn there in the hope of finding a pound note which I suspected I had dropped in the Square the previous day. I always was pound and penny wise, fortune foolish. It was the act of bending down to examine a piece of coloured sweet wrapping in a gutter that brought about my downfall. The motorcycle came to an abrupt halt and I hit my chin on the tank. Movement was impossible. It was as though I were in a strait-jacket but without the use of my legs. They were employed in keeping the machine upright. My shoulders were glued to the handlebars and my arms were stretched out sideways. With my feet I tried to edge the machine backwards but it would not budge. Why did no one come to my aid? Though my vision was restricted I could see the outlines of passers-by and there was no shortage of them. Then it came to me how much the average person dislikes to be involved. A man who falls in a fit instantly becomes a pariah and my ungainly stance might easily pass for epilepsy. That was it! I must wait for a doctor or the police.

The attentions of the latter might lead to an unwelcome outcome. The BSA had once been insured but never licensed. The scope of my driving licence was controversial. Explanations would be demanded. One's relationship with the law is coloured by how one attends to these things. Now my yoga-like stance led to reflection. I remembered as I crouched there how my father, an autocratic yet law-abiding man, had once told off a village constable for failing to do diligence. A gypsy caravan had appeared on my father's ancestral acres, in Norfolk where we lived grandly, and it offended his eye. He instructed the constable to have it sent smartly on its way. Nothing was done about it. My father decided to take the law into his own hands and called his agent for consultation. The agent was told to take a strong man with him at dead of night and to do what was necessary to punish the offenders. It was generally believed that my father, like the third murderer in *Macbeth*, went along to see the matter accomplished. It was. By morning the caravan appeared to have fallen into the local river.

But things had changed. When the blue-sleeved arm came to my rescue I felt far from autocratic. But he was a man with a sense of priorities, more anxious to persuade me of the dangers involved in the wearing of my coat than to point out that my Road Tax had expired in 1940. I talked fast and away from the point; he was smilingly sympathetic, even promising to let me know if my pound note was handed in to the Station. But in 1950 the pound was still worth something, and there wasn't much hope of that.

Some incidents were irresponsible. Though my job was a dead-end one and only a sinecure because of dishonest contrivance, it would have made sense to keep it until something better turned up. But it bored me to tears and boredom is something with which I can't cope. After the morning clock-in I had perfected a vanishing act so that I might escape the keen eye of McMaster who, if he found me, would set me to do some degrading task such as painting the workers' cabins or collecting Janetty's groceries. Janetty was a sawmill widow, a small, dark, ill-favoured matron, who occupied a cabin on a grace-and-favour basis. Her husband, a Newfoundlander, had died in macabre fashion a few months before. A bragging drunkard, he was often wont to walk along a sawbench until, by rising on tiptoe, he could straddle a revolving blade. On his final trip he had slipped on a patch of loose sawdust and fallen forward on to the teeth. It was said that no one who witnessed the resulting butchery was ever the same again but when Janetty was told about it her only remark was: 'Silly bugger', which was followed immediately by a claim for compensation. In order to pacify her, McMaster offered her a shed and a few basic groceries. Whenever I took them to her she made coarse passes at me and she was not a pretty woman. The whole thing depressed me and I determined to phase myself out of the job by reducing my attendance at the mill to one per day, the finishing time of five o'clock.

The men, put on their honour by me to start on time,

immediately took full advantage, production fell and I was caddishly betrayed by the worst of the malingerers. McMaster sent for me and five stormy minutes later I had rejoined the ranks of the unemployed.

Spring turned to Summer. In nearly a year the Bungalow showed great improvements but most of these had been internal. We had two pretty little bedrooms hewn out of the tough hardwood of the coaches, a nursery for the children, a functioning kitchen, electric light and even a telephone. But we had done little to the sitting room. The small firegrate fringed with flowered, glazed tiles and the wide areas of glass were scheduled for change. We cared to live neither in suburbia nor in a greenhouse, but money was sadly lacking and we had to make do. Essentially a summer house, we were able to overlook such things in the Bungalow in summer time, but the prospect of winter never left our minds.

We had begun to build our garden. Much of the ground had been used to dump rubbish and Joan insisted that every tin and broken bottle should be found and removed. We mowed the thin grass and gave it a little strength. There was a fence only where our piece of land fronted the road and men and beasts alike feel a primitive need to demarcate their territory. Some do it by an encirclement of urine, others by walls of steel and concrete but we decided upon a loop of 'backs' – the trimmings of round timber – which most sawmills are only too pleased to give away. Thus enclosed we found heart to improve our land. A state of privacy, the knowledge that one's domain has some protection against casual entry, is necessary to all except the unhealthily gregarious.

My wife began to plan the garden. First came the furniture. We built a flight of shallow steps in the bank below the Bungalow, using slab stones. Outside our bedroom window she decreed that a pergola should be mounted over which rambling roses might twine themselves. Her nature demanded the colour of flowers, their warmth and their scent, things oddly lacking in this monotone landscape of brown and green. The infertile soil grew only shrubs like gorse and juniper; to create a flower bed it was necessary first to dig a trench, then fill it with leafmould and as much loam as we could find.

We set up the pergola using stems of birch and arching it over with smaller sticks. It made a pleasant passage-way; the fresh young birch had brightly coloured varnished bark. We put some rose trees into the prepared beds and poured gallons of water on the imported soil, for moisture was hard to retain. May was dry with a cold east wind, June turned hot and clear. Even drought-resistant plants gasped for life while the sparse grass turned as lank and yellow as it had been in April when the stifling coverlet of snow had been first withdrawn. We prayed for rain.

It came, after the first thunderstorm of the summer. We had been warned that such storms in this area were often heavy. One of them at least had ended with tragic results. In June 1914 a huge storm had broken in the hills above the village. It was heralded by a gloom which was nearly as dark as night. A torrential downpour followed and the waters of the Baddengorm Burn, which passes under the railway line near the station, rose to ten times their normal height. Tree trunks, gravel and boulders, dislodged from the higher reaches of the burn, were carried down in the rush of flood water and piled up against the arch of the bridge. The surrounding embankment was soon washed away and the bridge's foundations fatally weakened. The driver of the train which presently came upon the scene could do nothing to avert disaster. The rails upon their crumbling bed were still in position. Under the weight of the engine the whole collapsed into the raging torrent and in the middle coach five passengers were drowned.

Our experience, small by comparison but still highly disturbing, began on a July afternoon. It had been a hot blue morning, the end of a series of hot blue days, but by early afternoon an impressive range of beautifully sculptured clouds began to build up above the mountains. Silently, inexorably, the thunder-heads heaved themselves up into the clear sky, then, silent no longer, they boiled and flickered while a harsh, halting crackle of sound wandered down the sky and burst in a host of conflicting echoes. In the forest the pines, exuding a sweat of resin, stood silent in a deepening bronze twilight. There came another staccato rattle, closer and more menacing. 'Heather, come here at once', shouted Joan, already lifting Richard from his pram, and the little girl tumbled from her tricycle and made for the safety of the house.

Over the Slochd summit the rain was falling. A long grey skirt trailed behind the quaking belly of the cloud. All at once it was around us. But overhead there was still a patch of blue; briefly the sun glared through it then vanished behind thickening mist. 'Come in, you fool', called Joan and I left my grandstand seat on the lawn and came inside. There was an odd tension in the air. We spoke in small voices as the children sat between us on our bed. A gasp of hot wind blew against the window, went by, and the world seemed to hold its breath.

There was a flicker of blue-white light. An imprint of the window appeared on the opposite wall. The glare was so intense that the room was robbed of every shade of colour. The children cried out and Joan buried them beneath a blanket. Somewhere in the house there was a sizzling noise. It was cut short by the bellowing roar of the thunder which made our eardrums ring. The electricity meter was just in my line of vision where it was mounted on the wall of the 'den'. At the next flash, through half-shut eyes, I saw a thick, vivid loop of white fire jump across the front of the unit. Then the house rocked; the carriage seemed almost to leap from the ground. I was frantically aware of the steel frame upon which we rested and guessed why we were receiving this special attention. They say that lightning never strikes twice in the same place but we, with our supply earthed unwisely to our metallic foundation, had become in effect a lightning conductor. Only Thor, that thunderous old god, would know what explosive pressures had been built up between it and the ground.

That afternoon the Bungalow received three direct hits

and the third was like the world's end. The whole building was lapped in a white flame. The telephone jumped from its table like a demented cat and flew across the floor while a puff of acrid smoke drifted from the ruined electricity meter.

In the silence that followed the echoes of the instant thunder we sat dead still, arms around each other and scarcely daring to breathe, while the muffled children whimpered through the bed clothes. The lightning went on flickering but the storm had moved away to the south. It was over. We began to talk quickly, even to make small jokes, and the birds in the forest, as though they too were garrulous with relief, set up a fine evening chorus.

A few welcome rain drops splashed on the steps. Shortly there was an urgent knocking on the door. It was our neighbour Will Calder: from his signal box he had witnessed the big strike, had seen the sparkling wave of fire pour over the Bungalow and was deeply concerned for our safety. We were able to reassure him and point out our damage. But we had yet to see it all. Later Joan called me from the bathroom: 'Come and see this', she said in a hushed voice, 'and idiots like you don't take it seriously.' Between the taps there was a broad deposit of carbon.

The public electricity supply had failed and I went to the telephone at the Station to report our plight. We lit our Tilley lamps. It came as a great surprise when later that same evening all the lights in the house were restored. I went to look at the meter. I could hardly believe that so burnt and battered a thing was able to function. Then I smiled cheerfully and went to report to Joan. 'I tell you', I said warmly, 'there's always a silver lining . . .'

'A silver what?' She looked at me incredulously.

'Lining, to every cloud. It's fine, only the meter can't record. It means free electricity until the next reading – and it was read only last week! We must look upon this as an Act of God.'

'I have married a lunatic', she stated flatly, 'we're nearly killed and all you can think about is saving a few pennies.

What *is* the matter with you? It would suit you better to take that grin off your face and ask a qualified electrician to see to an earth – if that's what's needed. You can do that when you tell the Board about the meter.'

Being the man she had married, we were able to enjoy about a fortnight's free electricity. Then the thunderstorms started up again. Having modified the earthing arrangements in my own way and to my own satisfaction I was quite sure we would now be safe. But apparently I had misjudged the power of the thunderbolt. The big flash came after a quick build-up: it was a single, well-aimed shot. We were back on the bed, the children back underneath the blankets. There was one bang, a tinkle and a smell of burnt bakelite. A brown cloud of smoke filled the 'den' and when it settled we saw that our days of grace were over. The meter had been blown right off the wall and one of the connecting cables had melted. And no more current came that way until a small man with a cunning screwdriver came to undo God's Act.

3 ❧ A Growth of Mushrooms

So with many alarms and few excursions our first summer in the valley of the Dulnain came to an end. We were a little older, our children a little bigger and our home had grown more sturdy. We had some jolly moments now and then but there were many drab days. Joan in her role as wife and mother was a paragon of the virtues but I was obsessed with trivia and undervalued time, which I have since learned is the greatest sin man can commit against his life. I started many things and completed few of them. I strode down the road of the weeks for the simple pleasure of striding but I had no idea of where that road might lead, while my wife, her mood fluctuating little between a determination to make something of our home and a sense of dislike and disappointment, planned, cooked, cleaned and brought up the children.

I seldom lost an opportunity to climb. If the weather was right and the urge strong upon me I would jump on my motorcycle and vanish for a long day in the Cairngorms. There I would be in Paradise, and it seemed strange to me that Joan did not respond to my accounts of it with more enthusiasm. Her only emotion seemed to be relief that I had come back at all.

One day in September she said to me: 'I'm not going to be able to stand this place in the winter. What are you going to do about it?' Her mood was neither kindly nor conciliatory and I saw that the matter was not going to escape discussion. Outside there was a sharp hoar frost which gave the world a brittle look and lent some weight to her contention. We sat and talked about it for some hours. We decided that the best thing we could do was to build a solid wall around the place. Both from an aesthetic point of view and from an urgent need for greater insulation, it was obviously the next step.

'I shall have to approach the Old Woman for some more money', I remarked, and she nodded glumly. She hated my dependence upon my mother, but had to concede the necessity. So I took the train to Inverness, which I did once a week, and spent an evening in the maternal presence arguing my case. The issues, regularly presented, were simple: further finance, or I should have to leave the area, probably emigrate, to find a career. This latter course was something that my possessive mother was most anxious to avoid. She wanted me around, on her terms.

With the fruits of my blackmail I ordered a load of concrete blocks, sand and cement. Characteristically I had left it all rather late. By the time the lorry arrived and discharged its load upon the lawn the first blustering October showers, half rain, half snow, were running in from the north. It was going to make the work uncomfortable but it also underlined its necessity. It was our intention first to raise a wall around the end of the coach which contained our bedroom and along the front of the nursery. The sitting room already had a low brick wall below the glass panels and its two ends were brick-built. The other end of the coach, the small bedroom, was to be reinforced in the same way and thus the wall would be continuous from the sitting room to the kitchen. Three-quarters of the building would then be enclosed. The other coach, where the bathroom was, would have to wait for time and money: it did, and was consequently never completed.

Work started on a dry October morning. I scraped away some turf and laid a few inches of concrete for a foundation. Then a single row of blocks was laid down. It was satisfying work, an adult version of the joy a child finds in building bricks. The concrete block is large and unfussy; its practical shape and substance makes it simple to use. No 'bonds' are necessary, indeed all that is needed for a presentable result is a straight eye and strong arms. Up went the wall as the showers began and the sleet turned to snow. It gave me a fine sense of racing against time, a dramatic heroic feeling that one was digging in against the weather.

Between the windows the wall went up to the level of the coach roof. Concrete lintels, cast in open boxes, were needed to crown the windows. Here the frost, against which I had been vainly warned, took a hand. It is fascinating to remove the shuttering from a shape cast in concrete and I am sure I am not alone in lacking the patience to wait until the mixture is quite set. After two frosty days and nights the mixture seemed as hard as stone. I pulled the nails from the rough boarding and revealed the smooth, clean surfaces beneath. How splendid the structure looked!

A few days later the weather grew mild. The thaw was like a thief in the night who robbed me of my work. We were woken by a succession of dull thuds: all the lintels had disintegrated. In our cosy single bed Joan turned her back on me: 'Oh my God!' was all she said. It taught me not to make concrete in frosty weather.

But by Christmas it was all finished. From one side our habitation looked like a house; even, perhaps, a small castle. At the top of the wall a line of blocks projected at right angles and supported another line upon their outside edges. This parapet was crenellated by gargoyle-like objects which enabled water to escape from the bitumen-ised felt roof of the coach. It worked with water but snow was a different matter. After a heavy fall this tended to linger in the gullies behind the parapet and when this happened everything became very damp inside, as one would expect to find in an igloo.

'I cannot go on keeping you – and Joan', my mother added snidely, as I sat with her one evening in the following January. 'I don't think you have even thought about work,' she went on, 'since that nonsense at the sawmill.' I was somewhat put out by her attitude. She had willingly financed the walling of our house but now she complained that that outlay, like others, had been forced upon her. I had to admit that my idle situation was indefensible since our house was now fit for habitation. But I intended to defend it. 'I have thought about work', I observed, 'even done something. I wanted to talk to you about it but you wouldn't give me a chance . . .'

'Ah!' she said, suspiciously, thinking that I had signed emigration papers, 'Would you like a gin and ginger? I think I might have a small one.' Since my father's death, even before it, she had tended to embrace the bottle, secretly and morosely. Yet she was not a drunkard.

I accepted a glass. 'Yes', I said stoutly, 'I wrote to the Ministry of Employment. They offered me something.'

'Where? In Inverness?' she asked hopefully. If this were the case she would try to persuade me to stay with her, only going home at weekends. Joan would be tactfully excluded from the arrangement.

'Well, it was in Inverness. But I don't think it would be suitable. Not really. They wanted me to train as a male psychiatric nurse. Up at the hospital.'

'Couldn't you do that? They might pay you very well.'

'It isn't quite me, is it? I don't know about the pay.'

'It would be something. Can you afford to turn it down? Florence tells me that if you turn down jobs they won't pay you Social Security Benefit.' Florence was but one of a series of peculiar young ladies of plebeian origin whom my mother espoused as lodger/companions. My mother had discovered the working class late in life and tended to make a meal of them.

'Not if you have a good excuse. I wrote and told them that I would be unsuitable. Recurrent melancholia, I said.'

She failed to smile. 'And what else have you done?'

'I put an advertisement in *The Scotsman*. Described myself as a young man of good intelligence and integrity, also appearance, who was ready to accept anything legal with good prospects. I've had four letters in reply. None very helpful, I'm afraid.' My mother was priming her mood, as one does a bomb, but with gin. To promote my own integrity I held out my glass. She waited for my explanation.

'The first one suggested I went into insurance. In Edinburgh. Training, car and two thousand a year. They claim it's very easy.'

'Well?'

'I'm too shy. You know I'm no good with people.'

'And the next?'

'To make cuddly toys. Round the fire at night. Wife a great asset, and even the children can help.' I noticed a pronounced sniff when I mentioned the word 'wife'. I went on: 'But they need an investment of five hundred pounds, to buy the materials. We couldn't afford that, could we?'

I paused long enough to assess her reaction. Had I not mentioned 'wife' I might have been home and dry. As it was she shook her head.

'The trouble is, they all seem to want an investment. There's this one about electric light bulbs with indestructible filaments. You buy the stock and a dispenser and set it up in a public place. But if we were to do it in Carr Bridge we'd soon run out of custom. Everyone would have indestructable bulbs. Even I can see that and I'm no business man.'

She agreed. 'What about the last letter?'

'From a society for the protection of homosexuals. Not my line at all. They want a secretary. Unpaid, unfortunately. No, I'm very much afraid it'll have to be the colonies for me.'

The threat, and the gins, worked wonders. Four hours later, as I left to catch my train for Carr Bridge, my mother said sweetly: 'Well, I know that you're trying. Why don't I give you a small cheque, just to tide you over?'

On my way to the station I bought an *Exchange and Mart* to read on my way home. It always provided spares for my motorcycle. Despite the comfort brought about by my mother's cheque the subject of my future employment still occupied my mind. I examined the propositions under the heading 'Business Opportunities'. One, in particular, took my attention. I narrowed my eyes, stroked my jaw reflectively and lit a cigarette. I reread the item with mounting excitement. Was this the answer to our problem, was this to be the future?

The night train to the South from Inverness reached

Carr Bridge at about a quarter to one. When it did so on that January night I could hardly wait to tell Joan my news. I sprang from the carriage, skidded along the platform and waded through the inevitable snow up to the Bungalow door. Then I burst in with a cry of triumph. My wife, confused at this rude awakening, did not know what to make of it, for at that time of the morning loud cries usually suggest disaster rather than salvation. She could hardly have been expected to realise that all our troubles were on the way out and even after a frenzied account lasting many minutes she was fully entitled to the question: '*What* are we going to grow?'

'Mushrooms!' I gabbled, all my misplaced energy channelled at last into an infallible idea. 'Mushrooms. The British Mushroom Company is the answer. Look! Read it' – here I thrust the paper under her nose – 'and you'll see. Hardly any outlay. They'll grow anywhere – in cellars, caves, darkrooms, even in the open. The Company will sell us the spawn and we need only straw and a thing called Kroppit to make up mushroom beds. They are easy to grow!' I paused to breathe.

'I know,' said Joan, rather soberly I thought, 'we used to pick basketfuls in our fields in Sussex. I love them. I expect there would be a local market, but would it be big enough?' She was warming to the idea.

'I hadn't thought about a local market', I said, 'but the Company will buy all our crop. They'd go by train straight to Covent Garden. We can start with one bed outside and as soon as that gets under way we'll put down another. For the winter we'll need a mushroom house. The Company sells blue prints for that; and there's an enormous price to be got for mushrooms in the winter.'

'And what about the money to start with?' asked practical Joan, 'there must be some outlay. I think it's a good scheme but can't we borrow something from a bank? I'd much rather be independent of the Old Woman. I'd get on much better with her if we were.'

'Probably, I'll try anyway', I said dishonestly, preferring

the idea of the soft option. I truly believed my mother would be offended if we showed too much spirit. 'Now I'll make some tea, and then we can talk about details.'

So we planned out brave new future until the slow morning came greyly in the east and big, soft snowflakes began to fall as softly as kittens' feet among the branches of the forest. When we finally woke it was to a fresh white world and it had grown very cold, but we had found a rosy flush of hope and we held out our hands to its promising warmth.

I told Joan that my bank wasn't interested and went back to my mother for help. The Old Woman was delighted. She had taken recent threats of emigration quite seriously and before I presented her with our new project she had sent a telegram saying: 'Good luck to you and your family in Australia.' She fired telegrams at us like poisoned arrows even though we now had a telephone. They usually demanded my presence, claiming illness or depression, and never failed to have a disrupting effect upon my relationship with my wife. I fear that this was a large part of the design.

But now she showed a real desire to help. In a way this was not unexpected, for the scheme, if it succeeded, would keep me nearby without a continuing drain on her resources. And I have no doubt that she had purer motives too. She was fond of her grandchildren but had less regard for their mother. Joan, volatile and independent, a bit of a Cordelia, would not be possessed nor undermined: therefore there was no lasting peace between them. At any rate, she made more money available, not stinting it, but it came with the warning that she could not help much more. This time I believed her and her sincerity showed me how despicable my position was. I determined to succeed. I did not see how I could ever admit to further failure after the tremendous build-up I had given the idea.

Of course, in the event, rather more cash was needed than 'the small outlay' which, to promote their business, the Company had said would suffice. I ordered a ton of Kroppit, five tons of straw, and enough spawn to sow an area of several hundred square feet. Then we would need to cover our bed to protect it from rain and sunshine. For this I bought a number of asbestos cement sheets which we would lay across bales of straw, thus forming walls and a roof. All that remained was to find a place where the straw could be turned into compost and for this the garage seemed ideal. It had a smooth concrete floor. Outside it I laid a wide slab with walls two feet high, like a shallow swimming pool. The garage already had a tap from which we would draw the necessary water.

To make compost on this scale was heavy work. To start with I loosened the contents of forty bales of straw and spread them as evenly as possible on the wide slab. Next I sprayed it for hours until it was saturated: then forked the whole into the garage in the form of a tight circle. This was built up in layers a foot thick when trodden down, with a thick dusting of Kroppit upon each layer. By the time all the straw had been used the stack was cylindrical in shape and ten feet high.

An important stage had been reached. We waited anxiously. For two days no change took place. Then the heap began to sweat and steam like a fat man with malaria. I pushed a special thermometer, purchased from the British Mushroom Company, into the heap and it showed a high temperature. So far so good. When it reached its peak the next day I knew that it was ready for turning, and that this must be done three times. The first turning was really strenuous. The straw, though softened by water and heat, was still tough and had to be combed apart. Following instructions I turned the whole heap inside out. In the close confines of the garage the clouds of steam produced a state of high humidity. Stripped to a loin cloth and running with sweat, my skin absorbed the fumes of sulphate of ammonia to such an extent that, despite regular corrective baths in Joan's most exotic essences, I smelt like an incontinent old horse for the whole period of the exercise.

The second turning, with the straw now dark brown and very friable, was much easier: the third, simplicity itself. By now the compost was an even dark brown in colour, slightly moist when squeezed, with an inoffensive smell and as easily torn as blotting paper. It was exactly as it should be. We were ready to set out the first bed, an area of fifty by eight feet with a depth of nine inches. For its site we chose a piece of flat ground below the bank on which the Bungalow stood. Using a wheelbarrow, the transfer of the compost did not take long; we set out the straw bales around the bed and roofed it with the asbestos sheets.

Before planting the spawn we waited for two days. Apparently the compost might heat up again to the point where it might damage it: but this did not happen. On a fine April morning we set about the final task, breaking up the spawn, which resembled Weetabix, into walnut sizes and pressing them into the compost at nine-inch intervals. It only remained to cover the surface with a thin layer of loam – to hold in moisture and support the fungi – before closing the lids carefully and keeping our fingers well crossed. Everything appeared to be perfect. As long as we could protect our bed from rain the mycelium should soon begin to run.

It was hard to be patient. After ten days or so I could not resist a sly glance. I carefully dug into a corner of the bed until I found a piece of spawn. My ensuing howls of glee brought Joan and the children to my side. No longer was it a dead and isolated lump; from its core curling white strands had moved into the surrounding compost. I hugged Joan excitedly while Heather and Richard, picking up our cheerful vibrations as dogs and children do, postured happily around us.

This early promise confirmed our ambition to build a house for the winter crop. Until then it had seemed an improvident move, for our means would not extend to such a project and the house would have to be built entirely on credit. But it had become the logical next step and a safe one: even a poor crop at high winter prices would pay for the cost of materials. Thus convinced, I ordered a hundred sheets of asbestos and many lengths of angle-iron. The floor was to be made of concrete. I was contemptuous of planning permission and ignorant of the dangers of asbestos dust (most people were in those days) and I worked non-stop from dawn to dusk for the rest of the month until the hideous edifice was finished. As a building it was quite the vilest-looking ever made. It squatted like a huge, grey shoe-box at right angles to the Bungalow, forming an L shape with the existing mushroom bed. Joan deplored its horrible appearance much more than I, for I was sure that in its dark, echoing interior all our best hopes would soon reside.

Despite these brave investments in the future – rather, perhaps, because of them – we had become ridiculously poor. It was only pseudo-poverty for we could not starve but I was done with maternal grants or even lease-lend and would only tread that path again in dire emergency. We reacted to this situation in our different ways. Joan would dress for dinner in the jungle, she is that kind of person; I am the type who in the face of misfortune immediately fails to shave. She contended that we should hold on to our modest standard of living until we had the means to support it: my fibres were so immoral that I advocated total retrenchment.

One morning I had the effrontery to suggest to her that we phase out the *cakes*.

The *cakes*, mark you, were symbolic of good living, and they graced the table each afternoon when the traditional English tea would be set out at four p.m. Naturally the children awaited this regular ceremony watery-mouthed and sometimes one or two neighbours, retired people we had come to know, would join us. It was clear that we were taken as young eccentrics, but it was not, thanks to Joan, the kind of eccentricity that implies poverty, rather an opulent perversity.

Unfortunately we could not pay for the cakes.

They came from Grantown on the bus, every Wednesday. Until the onset of this new impoverishment the baker's account had been scrupulously paid each week but now it fell into arrears. Since we could not settle the accrued dues it seemed wrong to cancel the service and we went on eating the cakes with a growing sense of doom.

In his first attempts to get his money the baker suggested politely that we might have overlooked his small account. Even then it was not small; it had built up into a good round sum, as might finance a banquet. Further letters came. They were so courteous that they made us deeply unhappy and soon we refused to open them. Envelope followed envelope into the burning heart of the Rayburn. It was wearing us down morally: God knows what it was doing to him. I cannot conceive how the matter would have been resolved as the stream of cakes continued unabated, had we not been blessed by a wonderful stroke of good fortune. It was a cheque from my father's trustees for fifty pounds, the balance of the cash I had anticipated in buying the Bungalow.

Joan and I sat down joyously like two children deciding what to send their little friends for Christmas. We didn't have that much to distribute and the area of distribution was large but we weren't going to keep anything for ourselves. We sent out five pounds here, five pounds there but first we opened the baker's latest letter. That dear man hadn't got beyond the gentle remark that we must have overlooked his small account which now stood at £24 18s 6d, the cost of over two hundred cakes and their bus fares. I would have been churlish just to send a cheque without explanation and in the exuberance of this righteous moment I wrote:

'I am deeply disturbed by the amount of your account. Although it in no way absolves me from responsibility I must explain at once that my day-to-day affairs are handled by a secretary who is at present on holiday. This misguided young man has, it would seem, extended his vacation at your expense, and that of others. He has committed acts of misappropriation of the blackest kind. I enclose my cheque in settlement along with my deepest apologies and the assurance that when, and indeed if, he dares to darken my doors again, this reprobate will face instant dismissal.'

The baker replied by return of post. With immaculate consideration he had expunged his tiny rebuke and sent his receipt on a clean billhead. He enclosed a short letter whose contents banished any misgivings I may have harboured about the essential goodness of human nature. He thanked me for my cheque and the quite unnecessary apology. He went on to ask my permission to observe that young men are easily led astray and added a request: would I find it in my heart to give the secretary another chance? He ended by saying: 'I am sure that under your just and firm guidance that young man will reinstate himself honestly in the community.'

Joan still buys cakes. Often we eat them with our morning tea, which is an old family custom of hers. There is a kind of which I am very fond and whenever I taste its sweetness I am inevitably reminded of Grantown on Spey and the most courteous baker in the whole, wide world.

4 ✤ *The Bad Angel*

At the stroke of mid-day on every weekday of that Spring 'Dunc the Stamp' would prop his GPO bicycle against our wall and bring us a handful of threatening letters. The 'Stamp' was a small man with a gentle face and pale complexion but he had a will of iron and an obsession about identity. Nothing would make him part with a letter until he was convinced that he was giving it to the right person, even when that person was well known to him. Only after repeatedly comparing our names to that on the envelope would he pass it over. More often than not, I should have been glad if he had kept it. I was fast beginning to recognise my creditors' typewriting and few of Dunc's offerings were received with much pleasure.

So it was nice to find a white envelope among the brown dross that our postman was meting out to us. The handwriting on this one was bold and familiar. I regarded it, after wresting it from Dunc's cautious hand, with pleasurable anticipation, a mood I wanted Joan to share. I took it to her and showed her the front. 'Do you know this hand?' She is good at recognising handwriting and marvellous at faces which is one of the many reasons why I married her. I have no visual memory and could never have been a spy. Now she said at once: 'It's Peter Randall.' She didn't seem awfully excited by it.

'I've been a fool', wrote the person she identified, 'but I've woken up. When I was demobbed my father set me up in business – a dreary job in a cosy Cardiff office. How I suffered! But no more! The great indoors is not my cup of tea and so it's back to Scotland and the mountains. There was a struggle with the old man but in the end he agreed, but with poor grace to give me a regular pittance while I learn forestry. Here's the punchline! I'm coming to Glenmore Lodge as a trainee, and you and Joan are going to see a lot of me from now on.

'Can I stay for a few days until I move in there?'

We had met him in the last year of the war. He'd heard that I was a climber and found me at my parents' home in Inverness. I was then at an RAF Motor Transport unit a few miles away and had wangled permission to live out at home where Joan, herself just demobbed from the WAAF, was pregnant with our daughter Heather. Randall breezed in one evening and introduced himself. He'd done some climbing and was keen to find a kindred spirit so we arranged a trip or two but it was difficult to make our free days coincide. Then came an unexpected chance. My section officer called for me one morning: 'Corporal Frere, I have been asked to release you for special duties. The O.C. Kinloss has a Sergeant Randall on his strength who is an experienced mountaineer and, I believe, a friend of yours. Randall is coming to us to do a small job and we want you to team up with him.' Here my superior gave me a snide smile: 'I think we can spare you because you have no job here since you burnt out the rear axle of that Coles Crane, but I won't rub that in. These things happen, especially if you don't check the oil. Now I'm going to ask you to sign for a Bren Gun carrier. Treat it, please, as if it were your own.'

'I will, Sir', I answered, wondering what all this was about. Were we being asked to put down some local insurrection? 'The thing is, Corporal,' went on the officer, 'we want you to bury some crashed aircraft. In the past five years a number of chaps have pranged in the Cairngorms and bits and pieces are lying about all over the place. Unless they're cleaned up we'll have endless reports and no end of trouble. You'll take six men with you, and the Bren Carrier is to get them as near to the mountains as possible. I don't suppose they will all be as keen on walking as you and Randall are!'

'Thank you, Sir', I said, feeling wanted for the first time in years. Since I had been turned down for flying duties because of some trivial ear trouble I hadn't had much interest in my progress in the war. As I trotted jauntily out of the M.T. office I failed to notice a Squadron Leader in Administration going in. He noticed me.

'Corporal!'

I sprang to attention. 'Sir?'

'Don't you normally acknowledge an officer? I suppose you have been taught to salute.'

'Extremely sorry, Sir. I did not salute you because I have no cap.'

'No cap, Corporal. Explain yourself.'

'It was destroyed, Sir. I used it to beat out a fire in the axle of a Coles Crane. I was afraid for the petrol tank. You see . . .'

'Is this insolence? How long ago did you have this fire?'

'Three days ago, Sir.'

'And still you have done nothing to replace the cap? Your honesty gives me no satisfaction. Go at once to the Stores and do not let me see you improperly dressed again.'

So Randall and I went to the mountains. For a glorious fortnight, helped by a team of elderly regulars, we hid broken wings beneath great mounds of stone, levered engines into deep gullies and tidied up the pathetic things like shoes and pieces of charred, stained clothing, until we had made the mountain tops innocent of tragedy. Then we gave the men a few days' rest, took a rope and got down to the serious stuff.

We were demobbed a few months later, at about the same time. Randall went home after promising to write about his post-war plans. In fact the letter which had just arrived was the first we had in three years, but we were to get used to his silent disappearances. He always had an air of sly mystery about him.

Joan was not as keen that Randall should stay with us as I was; she had an intuition that I might invite him to prolong it, for two climbers often become hard to separate. Also she had misgivings about him which I did not share but she put these aside and cheerfully made preparations for his arrival.

As a personality Randall was larger or smaller than life, depending on your viewpoint, so we light-heartedly prepared a fitting welcome. On the morning of his coming I climbed our electricity pole and hoisted my family's coat of arms which had last been publicly exhibited at one of the great Delhi Durbars. It rippled self-consciously in the light breeze, uneasy in its new function of proclaiming to the world that the Frere family were at home. Then we set off to the station carrying a short length of red carpet.

Will Calder the Signaller and his wife were used to us but the Station Master had the reputation of being a bit of a communist. When he saw the carpet he looked at it with suspicion. 'It'll no' go on the first train', he remarked , 'you'll need to hae' it wrapped and labelled.' I put him right. 'It's not going', I answered, 'we're using it to receive a Very Important Person. A friend of ours. Young Viscount Cardiff. I'm surprised you don't know that he's expected.'

'I dinny ken onything aboot it', said the Station Master.

A few minutes later the London train came to a halt, exhaling a great breath of steam. Few passengers alighted here at this time of the morning and if a door opened at all it was likely to be Randall's. It was! We ran forward and laid the red carpet upon the dusty platform. Randall sprang down upon it, roaring with glee. He had grown a beard and had an air about him: the false rumour about his identity seemed to have spread for two local men stood stiffly at attention while a housemaid from the nearby hotel experimented with a curtsey.

Randall rubbed his hands together in excitement and conversation burbled between us like a stream in spate. The train prepared to leave. 'No!' shouted our friend, 'hold it a minute!' The order was countermanded, giving him time to extract a motor cycle from the guardsvan. Joan looked momentarily put out and I heard her murmur: 'Oh, no, not another one.' She saw it as a further link in the chain which would be forged between us, another machine whose greasy parts would end up in the kitchen, whose wet sparking plugs were destined for her clean oven. 'Boanerges!'

proclaimed Randall, introducing it. 'Do you still have
yours, Old Man? We are going to have fun!' Passengers for
Inverness, impressed by the charming pageantry of the
occasion, smiled at us through the windows as the patient
locomotive spun its wheels and drew away on the last lap of
its long journey.

Joan had been right when she suspected that Peter
Randall might linger. She was proved so the very next day
when after a brief visit to his new employers he came back
with the lament: 'They can't put me up yet. There's a bloke
in my hut who won't be leaving for three weeks. I can't ask
you, Old Man, or you, Joan,' he turned to her, looked very
plaintive, 'to keep me that long.' I thought it prudent to
remain silent. Above the beard a look of speculation grew:
'Tell you what', he said, 'I'll try to find a lodging in the
village.'

'Don't be stupid', said Joan, 'of course you must stay
here.' She was only half laughing. He needed no pressing
on this point, and I was relieved that the decision had come
from her.

May was a beautiful month. Randall and I went almost
daily to the mountains. Apart from failing to accommodate
him the Forestry Commission did not seem anxious to avail
themselves of his services; he spent three days with them in
as many weeks. I didn't care. He was a good climber and an
excellent companion on the hill. We did some quite heroic
things. When the boisterous days were over we would come
back to a big meal, Joan, and Sibelius played loudly on our
old radiogram. Occasionally we would find the money for a
little drink. It was the sort of welcome home that conquer-
ing heroes should expect. Having a selective imagination
and more than a trace of self-centredness it seemed to me an
idyllic existence and one which might most happily continue.

And all this time our investment was growing. The
moment had come to prepare the compost for a second bed.
This one, also laid outside, might be expected to crop well
into September. After that, with the temperature falling, we
would have to grow the next crop indoors so I ordered

several more tons of straw and a further quantity of Kroppit to give us enough compost to fill the four huge shelves in the mushroom house. The growing area there amounted to more than twice that of the outdoor beds.

Very quickly it seemed to me Peter Randall's three weeks were up. One morning we found him packing his rucksack with gloomy, conspicuous intention. I was sad to see him go although it was clear that with Glenmore Lodge so near he would be a frequent visitor; our climbs would be curtailed but certainly not discontinued. I was aware that parting with Randall was no heartache for Joan so I was surprised when she said to me: 'You know, poor Peter's not at all keen to go.' Ah, I said to myself, I must play this one craftily. 'He must go', I affirmed in order to rouse her sympathy for the current underdog, 'it's all arranged, and having him here is a bit of a bore for you.'

'Well, I don't know', she said.

'How would he get to work? No, it's quite impossible', I answered, twisting the screw adroitly. I was a simple enough fellow but I had learned that some women are prone to argue against their own best interests and to get what one wants it is only necessary to reverse the point.

'By his motorcycle, of course', she said smartly, 'it isn't far.' When Peter Randall learned of his reprieve he tipped the contents of his carefully packed rucksack on his bed, rubbed his hands together, chortled joyously and gave the general impression that he was about to go round the bend. My own state of mind was much the same.

A few days later I had what seemed a brilliant idea. With the second mushroom bed now laid and spawned there would be nothing to do until the first one cropped. For this we had about three weeks to wait and to fill this idle time I thought I might get a temporary job. I asked Peter to enquire if there was a chance of any piece work at the Forestry. By using one motorcycle to carry us both we could share the cost of travelling and it would enable me to bring in a little money and halt the growing accounts which otherwise would not be discharged until the mushroom crop began to sell.

The Forestry Commission agreed to take me on as a casual worker. Randall was a trainee, with certain obligations. His father had made it clear that his allowance would cease at once if he treated his new profession in the same cavalier fashion as he had his former one. I was uncommitted, a thing I love to be, yet I almost had a sense of guilt each Friday when I took five pounds home for a week's muscular work spent in superb surroundings.

The work was varied, though somewhat repetitious. Sometimes we would be shown blocks of young trees and told to brash them. This involved the removal of side growth to the height of about six feet. We used bill-hooks with long handles and after a long day it could become a bore but the smell of the hot pinewoods was like a breath of heaven and our only tribulation came with the evening flush of midges. At other times we ditched, prizing out big blocks of peat with our wide, sharpened spades. Often, when supervision was slack, we sneaked away and made off at a jog trot towards the great ridge of the Cairngorms that shimmered in the heat above the last high line of stunted pine. We were both tremendously fit and could cover astonishing distances at very high speed but it would still have come as a surprise to our foreman to learn that between the hours of noon and five p.m. we had reached the summit of Cairngorm and been back in ample time to finish the work he had set us.

The two motorcycles were inexpensive to run but we had found means of bringing down motoring costs to almost nothing. Neither Boanerges nor Bizarro – a name concocted from the Spanish word for gallant coupled with the sound of BSA – were ever licensed or insured and since petrol coupons were only issued to owners who complied with the law we had to find our own fuel in the Black Market. Red Petrol, stained so for commercial use, was easy to find and we experimented with various bleaches without success. The penalties for its illicit use were severe and when they were not actually running, the motorcycles were kept carefully hidden from prying eyes. This imposed a nervous strain upon us and we cast about in the hope of finding a substitute fuel.

We settled for paraffin, a spirit of controversial legality and very cheap. It was also efficient: my motorcycle would run all day on a low consumption. Admittedly a few cupfuls of petrol were required to heat the engine on starting: one primed the carburettor with it and let in the paraffin when it was running briskly. It was only possible to start on paraffin after the briefest of halts and at the end of a run you turned off the tank tap and let the carburettor run dry.

The strange thing was that only Bizarro would take advantage of this exciting new break-through. Boanerges was a cool runner. It drank up the apéritif and rejected the rest of the meal. 'Too highly bred!' remarked Randall disgustedly as his sulky machine gurgled into silence. Despite some Heath Robinson modifications it never took to paraffin and we made it a policy to use it with 'red', but only at times when detection was most unlikely. Like most policies employed by indolent and carefree people it soon fell into casual use.

I had taken a morning off to attend to the mushroom beds. At mid-day I joined Peter Randall at Glenmore Lodge. Both machines were unavoidably in use when properly we would have ridden together on Bizarro. It was a very hot day and after an afternoon's brashing we both had powerful thirsts. Homeward bound and without more than a passing thought for the risks, we hid the machines behind a wall and turned into a pub.

We were on our second pint when my companion who had a view through a window said: 'There's the law outside. I think he's found the motorcycles.'

'Don't say that', I choked, spewing beer down my trousers.

'Filthy swine. It's true', said Randall. 'We'll go outside but don't hurry. We must appear relaxed and confident. Leave this to me. I'm a better liar than you are.' He was, actually, and I was only too pleased to leave a delicate situation in his devious hands. I finished my beer but all the joy had gone out of it. Then we sauntered outside.

'It's a grand evening, Sergeant', said Randall. The constable nodded quite cheerfully: he seemed pleased at Randall's flattering promotion. He said nothing until we had wheeled the machines out into the road and were preparing to mount, then: 'You boys running on red petrol, are you?'

'Sergeant,' said Peter Randall with such a brilliant touch of outraged innocence in his voice that I almost burst out laughing, 'do you take us for fools? I read a case in the *Daily Mirror* a few days ago. Chap got three months. Really, Sergeant! But we can't let you go away with the wrong idea –' He turned to me, 'Can we, Old Man?' Then referred to the policeman, 'I'll let you have a look.'

That's going much too far, I thought. But Peter was cool. He started to unscrew the petrol cap but it seemed too tight for him. 'Bloody stupid thing!' he said in sudden ill humour, 'we just don't know how to make proper machinery, do we? When I was in Japan last month,' he added in a voice of autocratic disdain, 'I saw things which would surprise you.'

'Ach, don't worry, I was just joking,' said the constable, impressed. He began to move away. 'For God's sake, let's get out of here!' muttered my friend, and I saw beads of sweat running down his face like guilty tears. Reaction was setting in. He jumped on Boanerges and kicked the starter hard. Nothing happened. He kicked again and again, muttering 'God, God, God' to the rhythm of his kicks. The policeman had come back to us. 'Sit on it, an' I'll give you a wee push', he said kindly. After ten yards Boanerges fired and raced away with the joyous staccato bark of a dog closing on a hare.

Fully aware of my dire straits, I yet found time to feel chagrin at Randall's desertion. The voice of Boanerges had already faded on the still air. I charitably assumed that Randall's sudden flight was prompted by the need to appear casual. It didn't help me much. Yet here was the policeman again, a man of inexhaustible good will, offering me a push. I declined it with an agonised smile and a joke: 'This one always starts!' In fact, nothing was less certain, and it was out of the question to go through the usual drill.

Yet a topsyturvy chance seemed to rule that day. Boanerges, who always started, hadn't done so: Bizarro, who couldn't be expected to, did, and on the second kick. It coughed deeply, spluttered and roared into life. I breathed a deep sigh and nodded my gratitude to the policeman. But he was invisible; everything was. It was like being inside a cloud. Bizarro, ridding itself of unvaporised paraffin, had poured out a smoke screen which would have hidden a squadron of heavy cruisers. It billowed out and upwards until it filled the road. A driver brought his car up short, uncertain where to go. Bizarro increased speed. A few moments later I glanced backwards. The vapour had begun to settle and through its upper layers the policeman's head had just emerged. It was too late then, to see his expression.

It was Joan who found the first mushroom. In my absence at Glenmore she had lifted an asbestos sheet and discovered a tiny white crown. By evening that one had become a hundred and as we opened up the bed the full extent of our success became apparent. The surface of the soil was evenly covered by a multitude of emerging fungi. They were like stars in a dark sky. Though small we knew how quickly they would grow and we were sure that within a week we would be picking for our first dispatch. The punnet baskets that had waited so long would soon be filled.

It was a good moment, our first commercial success in seven years of marriage. We looked at each other in speechless delight, then hugged like children. Peter Randall seemed impressed with our crop but he walked away when he saw me embrace my wife. He was uneasy at such displays and I supposed that he must have felt put out that for once I had neglected him. He helped us replace the asbestos sheets, ate his supper in silence and then went early to his bed.

Joan and I sat up late, and talked about it. As we flattered the future with our fine plans two small people in pyjamas crept from their beds and made a secret visit to the mushrooms. Heather and Richard were bent on confirming the story they had heard earlier. What they saw in the strong July afterglow must have convinced them of its truth for they burst in to tell us about it.

'Now we'll be able to have mushrooms every day, won't we, Mummy?' cried little Heather delightedly.

5 ❦ *Bob*

Peter Randall had become very glum. In the few days before we started to pick mushrooms he had little to say and his mien was that of a man who suffers great misfortune. It was impossible to guess at the origins of his mood. Like most self-centred extroverts he could send a ripple of merriment through a room or bring a chill to it according to how he felt, but his current wave of depression was so opposed to our own jubilation that we found it quite irritating. So, after a long spell of gloomy, nail-biting silence, when he suddenly announced his departure we uttered no word in protest.

We began to pick mushrooms on the first day of August and the evening train to London took away twenty baskets. The rate of growth was amazing. It was hard to believe that after a clean sweep of fungi we could be sure of finding, twenty-four hours later, as many, or more again, but day after day it was so and soon we ceased to wonder at it. At the end of each week the British Mushroom Company sent us a cheque, smaller than we had expected because we were now in the season of mushroom glut but no smaller than they had promised, and my banker smiled kindly when I visited the premises where formerly I had been treated as a pariah. Only with Joan's help was I able to work out a compromise between my two jobs. In the mornings before I rode away to the woods I would give the beds a gentle watering and dust them with a powder which prevented infestation with the grub of the mushroom fly. In my absence Joan did the day's picking, and in the evening we took them to the London train. But many mushrooms did not go to London: as beginners we were over scrupulous and anxious to please and only immaculate fungi crossed the border. The many that remained, rejected for the most tiny blemishes, were a challenge to Joan's inventive cooking and appeared at every meal in a wide variety of disguises. Little Heather's forecast had come true: now Mummy gave us mushrooms every day.

In the second outdoor bed the mycelium was running strongly in dark brown healthy compost. But the hub of the project was the crop in the mushroom house which would bring in a price per pound three times greater than that which we were now getting. The growing area was about a thousand square feet, the possible yield two and a half times as many pounds of mushrooms, the expected price eight shillings per pound: it was going to add up to something! But it was only a beginning. We were already speaking about a second house and after that there was no limit to our ambitions.

To give me time to prepare the huge amount of compost needed to fill the house I hung an electric light in the garage and worked throughout the night. It would have been sensible then to have left Glenmore: we had outgrown the idea of living on five pounds a week and my services were badly needed at home. Randall was a stumbling block. He showed such black depression at the idea of losing my daily company that I almost feared for his sanity! He was now persona grata again at the Bungalow, absence having made Joan's heart less unfond, and to do him justice, when he made his frequent visits he was always ready to help me with compost turning or any other jobs of the moment. He would never stay the night and after Joan had given him a large meal he would set out for Glenmore behind the torch which was Boanerges' only lighting equipment. Once his torch failed: he drove down a corridor of trees with only the light of a starry sky to guide him when, without warning, there was the sudden sound of an engine and another unlit motorcycle brushed by him going in the opposite direction. The story was pure Randall, and as such the accuracy of its details was suspect: but it made good telling round the fire.

The loading of the shelves in the big mushroom house was finished. Everything was going well. We had paid most of our debts and now I proposed to reimburse my mother's latest outlay. She grew so quietly frantic at my show of absolute independence that I thought it kinder to both of us to drop the offer.

The second bed was about to crop. I knew that I must soon leave the Forestry Commission whatever adverse effect it might have on Peter Randall's equanimity. I thought of Joan, picking mushrooms all day as well as looking after house and children, and I knew I must be with her as soon as possible. I resolved that as soon as the new crop appeared I would sever my connections with Glenmore.

In any case we were doing no good there. To punish us for our constant absences – more remarked upon than we had realised – we were made to do menial jobs under closer supervision. This engendered boredom and we retaliated in an orgy of lunatic pranks. In one week we crashed at full speed into a closed forest gate while racing the forestry lorry down the narrow Sluggan Pass, cut down the telephone wires at the Lodge in a hammer throwing competition – our hammer, being a six-pound felling axe, brought widespread destruction to the insulators – and caused suspicion to fall upon our fellow workers by submersing the Forester's bicycle in Loch Morlich while we watched his concern from the hidden crown of a tall pinetree. In my case this absurd brinkmanship probably stemmed from a subconscious desire to provoke dismissal but Randall's delinquency was difficult to analyse. He continued to insist that his father would cut him off short if he lost this job but he seemed to have entered into a self-destructive mood. It was never easy to guess at what went on in his mind.

The pinhead mushrooms, thousands of them, had broken the surface of the second bed. Joan and I stood looking at them. 'Well?' she said. I had not forgotten my resolution. 'I'll give in my notice to the Forester right away', I assured her. Then I rang Peter at Glenmore. 'I must leave at the end of the week. Let's take French leave tomorrow and do a climb: I was thinking of Glencoe. Then I'll do a few honest days' work as a going-away present to

Mr Fraser and after that I must attend full time to the mushrooms. Joan's wearing herself out and this is just silly.'

But the climb we did was not just silly, it was unbridled lunacy. We set out late for Glencoe – about eighty miles away – and started to climb in late afternoon. The September evenings were drawing in. We spent the night on a tiny shelf half way up a crag called the Church Door Buttress in pitch darkness and teeming rain, unable to climb further or to descend. At first light we fumbled our way off the precipice and raced for home, arriving there in mid morning to a distracted Joan. We were in a state of exhaustion and still soaked to the skin. After a bath and breakfast I wrote a short note to Mr Fraser saying that for personal reasons I must leave the job. I decided it would be civil to deliver it in person. Joan looked surprised: 'Why can't Peter deliver it for you?' she asked. I was stubborn: 'No, I must give it to him', I answered, 'and bring back Bizarro.' It was true that my motorcycle had been left at the Lodge overnight.

We were dead tired and our reactions slow. Riding pillion on Boanerges I nearly went to sleep. As we came to Aviemore we saw the forestry lorry parked beside a shop, Mr Fraser seated beside the driver. The instinct for habitual concealment, now no longer necessary, was still strong in Randall and he seemed to forget that this was the man we had come to see. 'Avoiding action,' he grunted, 'bandits straight ahead', and he turned Boanerges into a narrow side lane at forty-five miles an hour. The smooth tyres squealed like frightened rabbits and we went over with a crash. Randall was flung clear and somersaulted into the gutter. Boanerges spun like a catherine wheel, striking sparks from the road, and I spun with it for my feet were caught between the rest and the frame. I was painfully aware of a huge area of agony in my right leg and buttock. Suddenly a static black shape replaced the revolving sky and I felt a sharp blow on the head. For a short time, as they say in the best adventure stories, I knew no more.

When consciousness came back, as it did within seconds, I was being drawn feet first from underneath the forestry lorry. The forester was regarding me with a look compounded of relief, disbelief and anger. I had an urge to get in my news at once and made a painful effort to find my pocket and the letter of resignation but both pocket and letter were gone and in their place was a mess of grit-laden and bleeding flesh. My right trouser leg, shredded by contact with the ground, had been ripped off and wound round Bonaerges' chain, and it would have been absurd to seek the letter there even if I had been capable of reaching it.

Seeing that we were both shocked, and one of us injured, Mr Fraser contented himself with the remark that he would not expect to see me for a few days. To Peter he said: 'Mr Randall, perhaps I might have a word with you later in the day after you have taken your friend to a doctor.'

Patched up, but still in pain, I was helping Joan to fill some punnet baskets the next morning when the telephone rang: 'Old Man' – he was as bright as paint – 'How's the leg? I've some news – we've *both* got the sack. Actually there was quite a scene, old Fraser was really mad. He said we were a pair of bloody idlers and he was damn glad to be rid of us. So now I must go home and square it with my father. I haven't thought up a story yet but I will, never fear! Tell you what, why don't I spend the night with you and Joan, and take the morning train south? Keep the mushrooms company! And we'll have a party to celebrate my departure.'

Since this was something that Joan was still keen to celebrate she joined us willingly in the sitting room of the Carr Bridge Hotel that evening. My leg was as stiff as a board and felt as if it were on fire, and I hoped that the beer would not bring on the need for frequent trips to the loo: I had to pluck up courage each time I got up. But after an hour or so I felt less pain: alcohol, massively administered, is a fine anaesthetic. Randall too, was mellow, and we had reached the stage of making snide or witty remarks about anything that captured our fancy. Joan, disgustingly sober, was in quiet conversation with an elderly resident lady; every now and again she flashed us a cautioning glance.

Suddenly, on the main road two motorcyclists roared by, obviously riding in brisk competition.

'Oh, these young people', sighed the guest, whose own girlhood would have been spent in the graceful days of the horse and carriage, 'I am so worried for them. These motorcycles are so dangerous, aren't they?'

'It *is* dangerous', I broke in. Speaking deeply into my glass, my tones were muted and sepulchral. I added sadly, 'And who should know this better than I?'

Randall took up the theme: 'How true that is. No man of prudence, seeing my poor friend, would ever want to ride again. He is the victim of a motorcycle smash.' His voice was as hollow and doom-laden as a Greek chorus. The guest was filled with sudden sympathy and turned to me: 'Were you very badly hurt? I am so sorry: I didn't realise.' I tried to reply but Randall was firmly in the saddle.

'Yes, he is dreadfully ill.' He spurted beer into his glass and sucked it back in an attempt to simulate a death rattle, 'he cannot live much longer. His back is broken and his head is lolling on his shoulders. The topmost vertebra – ah! quite useless to him.' 'Shut up, Peter', said Joan, 'don't talk such nonsense. It's time we went home anyway.' He was undaunted by her scolding and delivered a parting shot.

'Madam,' he turned finally to the guest, 'though my friend is doomed and must soon leave us he will always be remembered with respect by decent men and women – everywhere – for what he did in receiving his injury. In sacrificing himself and destroying his beloved motorcycle – named, may I tell you, Bizarro, after the Spanish – he rid the world of a most evil thing.'

'What thing?' gasped the wide-eyed guest.

Randall would have graced the stage. His timing was immaculate. He placed his hand on my shoulder and you could almost feel the lump rising in his throat. For a moment words would not come, then: 'He ran over and killed – a Forester. Oh what public spirit! What a glorious thing!' He bowed gracefully, then offered me his arm: 'Goodnight, madam, I have enjoyed our conversation more than I can say. Lean on me, dear friend, it is not far to the door!'

Joan had fled. We could hear the echo of her angry footsteps going up the Station Road. I was quite drunk as well as crippled and I could not sit on the pillion. Randall suggested I drape myself across the tank. 'Then you can be a dead cowboy and Boanerges will be your faithful horse.' He was still as high as a kite.

We woke up late to find Randall packed and ready but with only minutes to spare before his train came in. He said goodbye to us in our bedroom, thanked us cordially and promised to write. From the window we waved him on his way as he pushed Boanerges up the incline to the station. After he had gone I felt depressed. In some ways he was not an admirable person but he had a sense of mad fun and he shared my love for the mountains. I wondered when we should see him again. Joan broke across my thoughts with the remark: 'Darling, isn't it good to be on our own at last?'

She was right, of course, but had said it too soon. 'I think that's rather unfair', I replied.

'Is it?' she said, still smiling: 'I'll overlook the compliment. Anyhow, don't grieve too much. He'll be back.'

This was the time when our mushroom production reached its highest peak. The packing room – an unconverted compartment in the east coach – was a hive of activity each afternoon and when the evening despatch had been effected a heap of sub-standard but still excellent fungi remained. Our personal ingestion had reached saturation point and we gave away the surplus to anyone who wanted them. So as September drew to its close we began to look forward to the crown of our endeavour, the time, now at hand, when we should receive winter prices for our abundant crop.

I had fitted an electrical heating system in the mushroom house, and recorded the temperature on the first cold

Autumn night. We should need a steady sixty degrees to keep growth vigorous and this would consume a great deal of current but its cost was well within our estimates. It looked as though nothing could intercept our wonderful spell of good fortune.

Now that I was freed from the necessity of earning a living elsewhere I found the time, and had the resources, to attend to the Bungalow's needs. Joan had long deplored the look of the glass frame that fronted the sitting room and she had designed a façade of large cast arches to take their place. These were on order but rather rashly I had taken down two thirds of the glass frame in anticipation of their arrival. Before the arches came, with a gaping hole in front of the building and the roof supported temporarily by sleepers, there was a night of very high wind.

We were asleep when the first sleeper worked itself free and crashed on the floor. The second one came down a few minutes later. By then I was out of bed and had switched on the lights. The room was filled with leaves and newspapers were swirling around but I saw that the whole weight of the roof was now firmly resting on the remaining baulks of timber and I was not particularly worried. I went back to bed and worked my way in beside warm and cosy Joan: 'It's not too bad', I remarked, 'but first thing tomorrow I must strap up those sleepers tightly. Make them safe until the arches come.'

'Is the mushroom house standing up to it?' she asked.

'I didn't bother to look', I answered, a little affronted that she could doubt the durability of my prize handywork. 'Of course it is. That place would stand up to anything short of a hurricane.'

'That's good then', she said comfortably, 'after all this excitement shall we have a cup of tea?'

So we did that, and enjoyed it: then we cuddled down and went back cheerfully to sleep, but before the last of the tea was quite cold in the teapot the hurricane came.

This time Joan woke me, her urgent hand on my shoulder. The bed was shaking. The wind, blowing into the house's open mouth, was one long moan. Strong as it was, it still seemed to gain in strength until it came to a frantic peak and then there was a splintering crash and the crazy sound of broken glass. 'That's the last window', I said, 'bloody hell!' and added with foolish complacency, 'well it had to come out anyway. I'd better go and see, I suppose.' I got out of bed and pulled on my trousers and a shirt, but Joan was on her way already.

'Where are you going?'

'To see the children, of course!'

'They'll be safe in the nursery. It's protected from the wind', I said.

She didn't answer.

I pushed against the sitting room door hard but at first it wouldn't budge. I thought that something must have fallen against it. Then it gave way and the wind elbowed its way into the room and knocked some books off a table. I switched on a light and saw not to my surprise that the centre of the last frame was just a jagged hole. The roof was pulsating but corrugated iron is flexible and it was fastened to brick at both extremities. There was no expensive damage here and I was about to say 'Oh well' and go back to bed when I saw what had broken the window and changed my observation to 'Oh my God!' On the floor, half covered by leaves, glass and splintered wood, was a large asbestos sheet and its edges were torn where it had been twisted from its securing nails.

I went to the window, not really wanting to look, and shone a torch. The mushroom house was being blown to pieces. Half the roof was already gone. As I watched another asbestos sheet was flipped loose and rose in the air like a bat to smash itself to fragments against the wall of the bungalow. Almost beside myself with fury and quivering with frustration at my inability to halt that wanton wind, I had not noticed that Joan had come into the sitting room. She is at her best in the face of adversity and taking comfort from her I found the strength to observe: 'It'll be OK as long as it doesn't rain. We can patch it up from the sheets from number one bed.'

At six a.m. the wind dropped dead, and it rained. It rained as if it never meant to stop. At ten o'clock as we walked around the ruins it was still streaming down and terminal damage had been done to the crop. The compost was just mud and brown straw. 'Would you bloody well believe it?' I asked, turning up my eyes to the wet heavens.

We spent the remainder of the day talking about it, adding up and more often subtracting figures, and wondering what to do next. We were still dazed for we had anticipated success so completely that it was hard to dismiss it as a dream. We had restored our local credit and had some money in hand: we might even expect some more until the outdoor beds, relatively undamaged as they were, stopped cropping. But to put a new roof on the mushroom house was a small item beside the cost of new compost and spawn: and in any case, starting now, we would miss the high winter prices. The risk was too great. We had been shown to be vulnerable and our confidence had taken a bad tumble. I had no job and, with winter just over the hill, no chance of getting one, and I was determined not to return to my mother cap in hand. I wanted such money as we had to last as long as possible. Without it I would feel like a naked man again.

So we decided to roof the mushroom house as cheaply and quickly as possible, then turn on the heaters to the maximum. Miracles can happen. And a heap of left-over compost in the garage was just sufficient to fill a space within the Bungalow itself – the guardsvan, used as a store – and there we might grow a small crop. Apart from this we had no plans. I sat back and waited, like Mr Micawber, for something to turn up, which is neither hard nor soul-searching when you are in your twenties and there are plenty of spare days ahead.

A few of them went by. In the garden bits of cracked asbestos lay all over the place, many of them half hidden under a high tide of autumn leaves. Joan and I had just started to gather up the debris when a cheerful voice hailed us from the road: 'Hello there, folks. Holy Old Smoke, what a mess. I'll give you a hand to clean up.'

We knew him by sight. His name was Bob Wilson, and he lived in the village. An ubiquitous and a busy man, he seemed to do a dozen jobs for a dozen masters and these all at once: it was unusual, on walking down the Station Road, not to see him on someone's roof, or painting a fence, or digging a garden. But we had never seen him at closer quarters or spoken more words to him than a 'good day' in passing.

Now he came through our gate. He was a man of middle height and sturdy construction but it was quite impossible to tell how many years had gone into the making of him. His face was a brown parchment, cracked and seamed by good humour and the Carr Bridge climate, and it wore an expression of original innocence. He sported a black tam o'shanter and a loud Canadian lumber shirt beneath an ex-Army battledress jacket which he now proceeded to remove. 'What happened here?' he asked and without further preamble he started in on the mess.

We told him the cause of our sorry state and it was a comfort to share the experience. 'Aye, aye', said Bob, 'yon was a hellish wind, right enough. I'm thinking yon roof wasn'a strong tied enough, and ye'd have been better to weigh it doon wi' stones. Like the old folks do in the islands. Onyways, you young people need cheerin' up, that's plain, ane I'll gie ye a hand now I'm to home for a bit.' This was kindly meant and it was no fault of his that I found his promise alarming. Even his advice would be welcome but our bantam-sized nest egg would soon be addled if we had to pay wages. But there was no stopping him and he went to work like a bulldozer. By the end of that day all the broken asbestos was neatly piled together and the ground had been raked smooth. We sensed he might be ready to go and I asked, with great misgivings: 'What do we owe you?' He brushed this aside: 'We'll no' worry about that. How'se about a mug o' char?'

His next actions in no way lessened our sense of obligation. He took over completely as soon as we were in the kitchen, made us sit down while he stoked the Rayburn against the evening chill and put on the kettle. The children were fascinated by this man whose pleasure in their company was obvious. 'Ony time youse folks want to go out,' he said as he bounced young Richard on his knee, 'just let me know. I'll come over and we'll have it dorg rough.' The children laughed in delight at the prospect of this exciting new game.

Before he went back to his 'cabin', as he called it, which was a wooden shed tucked away in the woods on the other side of the Station Road, Bob promised that he would return in the morning. He intended to help us make a garden for he had guessed that this was something necessary to a person of Joan's temperament: they had already discussed the matter between them. Joan had always wanted a rockery on the bank below the building.

'God', I enquired piously just before I went to sleep that night, 'how shall I find the money to pay this good man?' I did not know then that the saints render their expense accounts direct to heaven.

In the early morning we were woken by a peculiar sound. Our recent experience had made us nervous but we soon realised that this one was not ominous. It was the sharp ringing of steel on stone and through our open window drifted the strong smell of the Golden Virginia tobacco Bob smoked in his 'rolls'. We looked out to see our new friend industriously engaged in the traditional convict punishment of cracking stones. 'Youse stay where you are', he shouted as his hammer beat the life out of a monolith which had fallen long ago from the receding ice, 'an' I'll bring youse a cup o' char and toast.' It was clear that his promise of a rockery had not been an idle one. Already a dozen clean-faced fragments were lined up beneath the bank.

We worked together that day while Joan stood by with advice and kindly criticism and by the time the sun went down behind the signal box the rockery was well on its way. Bob was pleased to share our evening meal with us. Later, when he had washed up, he said: 'We got a plan to have it dorg rough, me and the children. Why don't youse folk go to the cinema? I reckon the kids and I'll get on fine.' It was a measure of the man's transparent integrity that after so short an acquaintance we were entirely ready to leave them in his charge. We took his suggestion with pleasure for we spent more time working in each other's company than playing and this was a small treat for us. But when we returned later, to a blazing fire, a steaming kettle, happily bedded children, scrubbed kitchen table, polished nursery floor, washed dish cloths and other domestic chores immaculately effected, it was clear that something had to be established. 'Bob,' I said when Joan had left the room, 'it can't go on. It must be clear that I'm not a rich man. You've no idea how grateful we both are to you for your help and we must talk about wages. I don't think I can –' and then he interrupted me, as he had before: 'We'll no worry about that. Money's no use to me onyway. If I get m'grub and a bath now and then, that's wages to me.' Then he added, with that broad innocent smile, 'It's no loss what a friend gets', and in that short phrase was summed up the essence of one of the most unselfish men it has ever been my privilege to meet.

6 ❧ Interim in the Cold

Apart from two days it had been a wonderful autumn. By the end of October only the birches were russet; the beeches and sycamores were just touched with yellow while the oaks refused to recognise the dying year. From the witches' rowan the berries hung like great drops of blood, sure sign, the old people said, of tribulation to come, but we had already experienced ours and it was a bitter pill to swallow. Just two exceptional days in the midst of this season of bland weather! If they had been written out of the calender how different our fortunes might have been!

As it was we earned a little money from the outdoor beds for a few more weeks. Three-quarters of the growing area had been inundated but what remained gave a steady yield. The heaters in the re-roofed house did their best but the spawn was drowned. We shut off the electricity, put it down to experience (not an allowable tax deduction) and called it a day. But there was a doleful postscript yet in store. In the guardsvan the compost had failed to heat at all but we spawned it in due course, automatically and rather listlessly. As we had feared nothing happened, the spawn remained inert and finally rotted away. Disgustedly I turned off the heater and shut the door on it but weeks later when I came to shovel out the compost I found a very strange thing. Bang in the centre of the bed was a gleaming white button mushroom which soon became a peerless fungus, large, perfectly shaped, its gills a lovely pink. It stood proud and solitary, like a revolutionary leader who awaits popular support: but none came. There was a symbolic quality about the beastly thing, its singleness was a blatant statement of our failure. We would not eat it. Presently it grew brown and old, toppled over and became dust. Only a bold man, one careless of his life, would spend time in the guardsvan for it held the threat of neuremyces, being filled with deadly spores unknown to science, and we feared that the Curse of the Pharaohs might fall upon us too.

That autumn lived on borrowed time. The mild hazy days continued unabashed into November without a hint of sleet or snow: the nights were free of frost. The Bungalow, with three gaping holes where windows should have been, had become a fool's paradise, or a volcano, formerly famous for its regular habits, which had lost its wits.

On the fifth we lit a small bonfire to amuse the children and fired a few rockets into the wood. The gods who arrange the climate seemed to take this as a show of defiance – it was not meant to be – and let loose, over the next week, all their restrained vindictiveness. In quick succession came rain, wind, sleet and snow, and the snow had the look of an unwelcome guest who means to stay. With the new moon, came the frost. That frost was something which had to be felt to be believed.

Bob and I, rather belatedly, stripped our boundary fence of its wooden backs and nailed them across two of the windows: to the third and centre one we restored a glass frame. This kept some heat in the house but the room was still much too cold to sit in and we lived in the kitchen. To keep the Rayburn constantly alight was imperative, a matter of survival, and we attended it with the care and deference which Olympians show their flame. In matters of fuel it was an omnivore; it liked coal best and wood was its second choice. The former especially was a problem, as was anything which had to be paid for, but Bob, the great provider that he was, showed us a way round that.

Less than a mile from the Bungalow the railway line swings right into the Spey Valley and hereabouts, for no very obvious reason, huge lumps of steam coal used to fall out of the engines' tenders. To this point, trudging through the snow, we would make a daily pilgrimage and come back in due course with as much as we could carry in two sacks. But, as might be expected, our prospecting soon attracted public interest and since we were not in a position to stake a claim to it others came with the same idea and took away our profit.

We turned to wood for fuel. Bob who had spent some nomadic years in Canada knew all about timber and what species was best for burning. He had a rare knack of detecting resinous deposits in the hearts of old, dead pine trees and strong shoulders on which to carry home his prizes. He showed us how to mete out this explosive substance so that in conjunction with less oily woods it might make a right royal blaze. It all but melted the firebricks in the Rayburn and inspired Joan into remarking: 'Wouldn't it be nice if we could build the fireplace in the sitting room? Now that we have this stuff to burn . . .'

I knew, and Bob was beginning to know, that such gentle-seeming observation cloaked implacable intention. We might get away with it for a few days but this project would not die a natural death. Rather than risk increasingly stern reminders we slunk out into a blizzard and started to search for suitable stones from beneath three feet of snow. Then out came the sledge-hammers and wrecking bars and we started to rip the small fire grate, the pride of suburbia, from the wall.

Everywhere we go, or have gone, Joan designs things. She loves to create fireplaces: it is one of her functions in life. This was her first, I think, and it was built in a heroic mould. Bob shaped the stones with a craftsman's skill and, not to be outdone I crowned it with two pillars of cast concrete. The thing was vast, cavernous and any ox, once having come to terms with its fate, would have chosen to be roasted in it simply for the prestige it offered. When the cement was dry and hard we lit a fire of red resinous blocks in it. At the moment of striking the match the temperature in the room was twenty-nine degrees Fahrenheit – three degrees of frost, and chilly for June, as Bob remarked cheerily – but half an hour later it was rising steadily and when the conflagration had reached fire storm proportions the astounded thermometer lapped the sixty degree mark. What a success! we said. Good heating in these northern

latitudes infers opulence and when we sat in lordly comfort
in front of this great blaze it was easy to forget our boarded-
up windows, shrinking bank account and the bitter cold
which lapped the world outside.

But soon demand exceeded supply. To find suitable
timber Bob had to go further and further into the forest
while our excursions along the railway line had become
utterly unrewarding. The situation had begun to look
extremely bleak when Fate, smiling upon us for once, sent a
bonus.

One Siberian morning I was fetching the milk from the
gate – it was so cold that in little more than an hour the caps
had risen from the bottles and stood on long pillars of ice
cream – when I saw our neighbour Willie Calder, the
signalman, running down the Station Road, his breath
streaming behind him like smoke. 'Anything wrong?' I
shouted, for I knew that his wife was not in the best of
health, but he waved his hand to show that all was well at
home and jabbed his finger in the direction of the distant
Slochd summit, the high point of the railway line north of
Carr Bridge. 'Coal wagons have broken free on the hill,'
was his shouted rejoinder, 'we'll be shunting them into the
hole.' The hole was a small gulley beneath the station. It
sustained some scrub, was littered with domestic rubbish and was scratching ground for the station master's
hens. It was also a grave for runaways, with catch-points
fifty yards up line and a short length of rail aimed at its
centre. On a single line such as this, it was a necessary
provision.

I dashed back into the Bungalow to tell Joan about it.
The promise of drama excites me like alcohol and I was
quite high. Bob, who should have been with us to savour it,
was somewhere in the backwoods hunting resin. Joan, an
anxious mother, immediately thought of the children:
would the impending crash frighten them? Despite my
claim that the experience would be a rewarding one she
insisted that they waited in the bedroom until it was all
over. 'Spoil sport!' I chided her, but only when she was

satisfied of their safety would she join me on the steps outside for a grandstand view.

At first it was very quiet. Then we heard the sharp clatter of points and the thud of the signalman's lever. The executioner was testing his trap. Then the sound of the runaway trucks, still several miles away, became audible and soon increased in strength. It was a thin, strong whine punctuated by the clunking of couplings, the grunt of the Gadarene swine, swans singing before they died! Within minutes they came into view, rushing headlong, joined together like soldiers advancing to death, hand in hand. There were six of them and they were going very fast.

They went into the hole one after the other, writhing and twisting on their links, and the crash was a long splinter of sound. The ground shook and a board fell out of the Bungalow window. Above the hollow a mushroom cloud of coal dust darkened the sky. Then again all was silence except for the outraged clucking of a few hens from the station master's decimated flock.

I went to look. Joan wouldn't come. The scene was one of absolute destruction. The sturdy wooden trucks were splintered and wheels and axles lay all around in a matrix of the best steam coal. Slowly, grinning to myself, I made my way back to the house: I felt like a man who has found favour with his God. Joan, a little white and shaken, met me in the sitting room. 'Well', she remarked, 'you've had your excitement for the day. Do you think you could find something to put on the fire in here? It's nearly out.'

I gave her a passionate bear-hug in reply.

For the next fortnight Bob and I were on night shift. At the end of it the garage was filled to the roof with coal as was every other vacant space around. Though strict moralists might call it pilfering this ploy was not immoral for British Railways did not intend to recover any of the coal but merely to bury it in order to avoid continual trespass on their property. This, considering the state of austerity in the country (and more specifically that in the Bungalow), was the true wickedness. Employees of the railway were strictly forbidden to help themselves though their own ration of coal was far from generous. The night after the incident we had found the station master with two large sacks. In the light of my torch his eyes showed a shifty look as he lamented: 'Just picking up my dead hens, half the buggers are gone.' He withdrew a fowl which looked like a monstrous blackbird and dumped it in one of the sacks. By the time he was ready to leave we noticed that he was hardly able to get it off the ground. 'I reckon there's more than birds in yon', remarked Bob, in an undertone, 'or else they've put on some hellish weight since they died!'

Eventually B.R. carried out their threat and sent a team of men and a crane to remove the springs and axles and bury the coal. They were welcome to the ironmongery, we had no use for that, but we were grateful that they left the wooden bodies in a pile. The splintered bits made excellent kindling and we cut the larger bits up into logs. There was, in fact, no coal left to bury. Again Bob was to have the last word: 'Holy Old Smoke', he remarked with his most fetching grin, 'I reckon we ought to send them a bill for cleaning up. It's us who's done all the work.'

At any rate it was a timely event for it happened shortly before the onset of the most ferocious cold we ever experienced at Carr Bridge. For three nights after three brilliant blue days the temperature dropped steadily lower. At noon there was still ten degrees of frost and when darkness came even the fire-storm in the sitting room was unable to hold its own and we rotated ourselves vertically against the flames like pieces of meat on a spit. By the fifth night the mercury in our thermometer was no longer than the tip of a lead pencil and a small wind outside was lifting little whorls of snow in feather-down dances.

Bob was now living at the Bungalow: he had moved into the old mushroom packing compartment. He came into the sitting room with two bags of coal, one of which he emptied into the fire, and remarked: 'Jeese, it's cold. It was like this in Alaska.' I went outside, curious to find out how it had been. As I opened the door the deadly chill made me choke.

My eyes watered and there was a sharp stinging pain in my nostrils. I spat experimentally but this famous test of low temperature did not succeed, much to my surprise, and the spittal splashed rather than tinkled on the stone step. Nevertheless it was a hard gob a second later. I studied the thermometer: it registered forty-four degrees of frost.

A few months later, in the Spring of 1952, my second book was published: my first had been printed privately, which is a different thing. I had started to write *Thoughts of a Mountaineer* before the war and for so long a gestation period it turned out to be a puny infant. Yet I saw it as an achievement and it swelled my head if not our bank account. Even so my advance of twenty-five pounds *was* twenty-five pounds in those days, and it was a pity that it was never covered by royalties.

After making the usual deductions for current debts Joan decided that we should give a publication party on the left-overs. There was a hospitality imbalance between ourselves and people who had invited us out throughout the winter but Joan had felt misgivings about the effects of cold upon the less robust of our friends and had postponed her invitations until the weather should warm up.

Now it had, and other things being as equal as they ever would be she decided upon a date. Soon she was discovered sitting at a table, writing. It was a list of things which are needed to mount a full scale dinner party and its scope winded me. 'That's a lot of stuff!' I remarked meanly.

'It is,' she replied quite unabashed, 'but we don't entertain every day. Not even every year, come to that. If so many things didn't have to be replaced it'd be easier.'

'What things?' I cast down my eyes but hers were filled with accusation. She didn't have to spell it out for she saw me flinch at the memory of silver entombed in bed-rock concrete and many innocent household utensils used illicitly in the building programme. 'Oh yes. Well, I suppose . . . But where's the money coming from?'

'That's your problem. We agreed to have a party and if

I'm to give it I shall do it properly.'

'Of course. But really! Smoked salmon! Wouldn't sardines . . .?'

I was withered by her glance: 'Don't be fatuous, this isn't the moment for it.'

As it went on, and it did for some time, a certain heat entered the discussion which Bob, not far away, couldn't help but hear. It was one of the many great things about Bob that we could fight in front of him without embarrassment. We often referred to him but in this case it was hardly necessary: we rocked the house with our complaint and it was on a familiar theme, the gap between ways and means. Instead of oil he poured tea on the troubled waters of our problem, discovered cigarettes in a secret store and improved relations. But in the morning he dropped his own bombshell.

'Youse folks'll have to do without me for a few days.'

'Bob!' said Joan, struck dumb. The date had been arranged, there had been one hundred per cent acceptance rate to invitations: little more than a month remained. He couldn't go away now!

'You can't go away now, Bob', she said at last, in great alarm. 'What about the cleaning? And you promised to be butler at the dinner. You must help . . .'

'Holy Old Smoke, Mistress Frere,' he answered her, but not without a smile, 'it's high time I hit the road for a bit. But I'll see you right for the party, never you fear.' Without more ado he put on his old army greatcoat, stuck his tam o'shanter on his head and slung his piece-bag over his shoulder. Then he hit the road. It was like a night-light going out.

Three weeks went by. At their end Joan had finally decided that I was no help in the preparation of the Bungalow for the august occasion. I was sent to get wood – we still had about five years' coal – and when I returned with a log on my shoulder there was Dunc the Stamp delivering a telegram from my mother. It said, shortly: 'Am very ill indeed. Come at once.' I looked at Joan: such perverse self-indulgence on my parent's part usually provoked a storm. But she merely said: 'Go on then, if you hurry you'll catch the three-forty train. I have plenty to do here and you're no help.' I did as she bid me and spent an acrimonious evening threatening to leave the country forever.

When I came back after midnight the lights were all ablaze and Joan was still at it. When faced with a deadline she can be very brisk but I found it hard to believe that any single person could have wrought such a transformation. The place was almost indecently clean: its immaculate state made me hold my breath in case my exhalations might fog the polished furniture or blur the windows. I took off my shoes in the mud outside. 'Somebody came to help?' I asked.

'No,' she said seriously, 'not ordinary people. I had the faeries in. There were dozens of them. They left just before you came.' This mood of whimsy lasted until, on retiring to bed, I thoughtlessly threw my shirt down on the floor. 'Hang it up,' she said, 'can't you see I'm trying to keep the place tidy? And, by the way, I hope you've found some money. We must go to Grantown tomorrow and do some shopping.'

I had to admit that my best efforts in that direction had not been blessed with success. Joan boiled up at once: 'What can you let me have then?' she fumed. I told her. 'Well, you can cancel it then. What do you expect me to do on that?' I was still explaining the financial situation the next day when there came a knock at the door.

It was Bob. He looked tired and dirty. We put our contention away in relief at his return. He gave us his usual greeting of 'Hello folks' and added, after an admiring glance round the gleaming kitchen, 'Mistress Frere has been busy. We'll have a cuppa, then I'll get on outside.' He plunged his hand into his greatcoat pocket and pulled out a wad of notes. He thrust them at Joan: 'This is for my keep', he said, 'an' it'll maybe help a bit with the party.' 'Oh no, Bob,' she said softly, 'I can't take this. You've been out working, it's your money.'

'Nonsense,' he replied, 'money's no use to me. I must pay for my keep. But if you don't want it,' grinning now, 'I'll give it to Master Teddy.' He offered a fiver to our son who was too overjoyed to see his dorg rough companion to grasp its vast significance. The whole amount was several times that, the hard-earned fruit of overtime work at the sawmill.

To borrow a phrase from the world of the theatre, it was all right on the night: excellently so, thanks to Joan and Bob. A great fire crackled in the sitting room and candle-light helped to soften the harsher features of the conversion. Even the backs, rough planks that kept out the night, had turned into pieces of rustic tableaux and the coaches had become an integral part of the house, as though to that fabric born. Bob was urbane, the perfect butler in all but uniform, as he presided over a table loaded with fine things to eat and drink.

Our friends were the kinds of people one finds, with individual variation, in any residential village. Here was the elderly lady artist, the fetchingly snobbish Scottish major, the son and heir of the local big hotel, two maiden ladies who fought a losing battle against dry rot in an old house they had inherited, the bearded, quiet man lately out of India and Jim and Shiela Wilshin who had become our good friends. And a few more.

I watched the Major's lady making her way to the powder room (the loo in the east coach) and I knew by her expression that she was impressed by her surroundings, quite unaware that her journey took her through two old pieces of rolling stock and hard by a guardsvan in whose gloomy cavern lay a ton of rotting manure. The Major himself, mellow with port and a brace of Drambuies, said warmly: 'You keep a good cellar, Frere. That port! Brought it from your family home, did you?' It had, in fact, been purchased in Grantown during the previous week, but since he had gone to some trouble to find out, from Burke's *Landed Gentry*, that as a boy I had enjoyed some privilege, I felt it would be unkind to deny it. He went on: 'What a fine woman your wife is!'

'Isn't she?' I confirmed.

Indeed, beautifully done up, Joan looked splendid: I decided that I'd have her for the next course. The Major was not finished: 'And Wilson!' Here his eyes looked avaricious. 'Wish we had him. Can't even get a decent skivvy here. Your man's a marvel. Seems to be able to do everything.'

I laughed sternly. 'Hands off, Major. Bob's ours. He's our oldest retainer. A remarkable person', adding a further accolade as I remembered where our cellar had come from, 'and I think there aren't many like him.'

When the other guests had gone Jim and Shiela stayed on for a final drink. Bob had stoked up the fire with two great crackling logs and retired to his compartment.

It was good to relax with a well-filled belly and a head hot with drink in the company of friends, but watching the Wilshins made me maudlin. They seemed so comfortably successful. We knew that they'd had their trials too but now they were on the right road and their guest house was making them an increasingly good living. Bully for them. I wasn't exactly envious, but what did they have which we hadn't? At which junction on the bewildering road of life had I taken the wrong turning?

Jim Wilshin must have read my thoughts. He was a man of high moral scruple and did not care to see people burying the life talent.

'What plans have you for next year, Richard?' he now asked me in a gently reproving voice. 'Shall you go on with your writing?'

'I can't afford to, Jim. Not on its own. I'll have to find something that brings in money and still leaves me time to scribble.'

'And climb?' he suggested, for he knew my fatal weakness.

'Well, yes. That too. Really I'm in a bit of a quandary. I'm trained for nothing and we can't lay our hands on any worthwhile capital. So what do I do?'

He gave this some thought. The answer was as obvious to

him as it was to me but he knew a stubborn man when he saw one and did not offer it. Nor did I want to hear it. One hates being rebuked for an indulgence that one is powerless to resist. After a short silence he said: 'Perhaps I shouldn't suggest this for it's a modest little scheme. It couldn't expand in the way you hoped your mushrooms would, not under present restrictions, but it would bring you in something. And it would leave you plenty of time for other pursuits and for your writing, which I think is important.'

'I haven't much confidence in my writing', I said sadly.

'You haven't much confidence in anything you do', said Jim with unusual heat, 'if you'll accept the opinion of an older man. That's your trouble. And you're too dashed fit! As long as you're using that sturdy body of yours you're happy. Climbing mountains, turning over heaps of manure, shouldering logs – you feel so good at the time you've not a thought in your head for the future.'

What he said was quite true. I asked him about his new idea.

'Well, it's poultry. Not a farm, obviously, but small units with a quick turn-over. Two things would recommend it from your point of view. You have your mushroom house which would accommodate the brooders and the cost of the brooders themselves is the biggest lay-out. They don't cost much. The catch is, you must look around to find the food for them, for the day-old chicks.'

'What worms, and things like that?'

'No you fool', he said tolerantly, 'it's called "growers mash" and is strictly rationed. Only accredited poultry farmers get it. You have to look around.'

'Jim', I said, 'you speak familiarly of this. Have you done it?'

'I'm doing it now. As you would know if you came to see your friends more often instead of forever tramping over the Cairngorms. Joan's seen our brooder house and she thinks it's a good scheme.'

I turned to her. She nodded. I said to Jim: 'I'm interested, tell me more about it.' He explained: 'I buy day-old cockerels a hundred at a time, very cheaply, put them in brooders – I have four – and fatten them for six or seven weeks. By then they usually weigh one and a half pounds each and are ready for the poussin market. It's a luxury trade and as such would be frowned upon in these days of austerity: but that disapproving old sobersides Sir Stafford Cripps hasn't noticed me yet! I have a butcher friend who gives me twenty pounds for them when he takes them away.'

'Twenty pounds – each?'

'No, idiot, for the batch of one hundred.'

'Oh', I remarked from a fallen face.

'It's still good money. It helps us with the overdraft in the winter. How about coming to Struan in the morning and I'll show you the works?'

'We certainly will.' The butterfly of hope was emerging from the cocoon of lassitude and it was a strong insect. My face lit up as my spirits bubbled like the wine which sponsored them. Jim saw the transformation and remarked: 'Don't go mad over it, though. With us it's just a sideline but one which helps. You should treat it like that too. The food supply limits it and if things get better – though Heaven knows I don't see it under this government – the big boys will swamp us. So go easy, old chap!' I didn't hear him for already I could see them: hundreds and thousands of tiny fat birds, roosting all over the bungalow; birds in boxes instead of mushrooms in baskets; birds going away, money coming back. More birds, more money. The infallible equation.

I smiled at Joan. She smiled back. Soon she'll be smiling even more brightly, I thought, with long holidays in the sun or a cottage in her chosen countryside. My mother will be subdued and I shall be free to climb my mountains without any sense of guilt at all!

7 ❧ Of Politics and Poultry

So we learned about chickens and for the next year or so our working lives revolved around them. We had some good moments and we found many friends beneath the feathers. I shall not forget the morning when Joan and I opened our first box of day-old cocks. They had come from a farm in Perthshire by train and we met them at the station to ensure that they might be released from their cramped quarters without delay. A newly-hatched chick can only live on its own reserves for about twenty-four hours and after that it needs to be fed.

'Oh! Aren't they sweet!' said Joan as she lifted a tiny yellow bird out of its crammed box and put it in our brand new brooder. It stood for a moment beneath the radiant-heat lamp before making for its tray of starters mash. Soon it was joined by ninety-eight companions: only one had failed to survive the journey. It lay, as thin and flat as a leaf, in the dry hay of the box. It was rather pathetic.

A week went by and the birds began to grow. Two weedy specimens stood with drooping wings and a disinterested air, voiding a white stool until they fell down dead and went to heavenly free range. In their swift passing we saw the finger of doom but Jim, answering a frantic telephone call, told us to compose ourselves for it was quite normal to lose one or two like that. And indeed apart from such momentary shocks we were not worried, for in terms of outlay and sustained preparation this scheme was a treat compared to the mushroom project, yet promised more immediate returns.

At about this time our daughter Heather, aged five, left us to go to a boarding school. This event, paradoxical in the light of our own circumstances, was made possible by a clause in a Trust deed. We both hated to part with her so young and missed her badly, Joan especially, but it was Joan who had proposed the course of action. She was determined that her child should be spared a full-time involvement in the insecurity arising from my experiments in living, contending that what might seem fun in the holidays could be destructively confusing to a young mind if continued all the year round.

We took Heather by train to Perth and there met the Lady who ran the establishment. Only a few words were needed to establish rapport between us. We found that Seggat School was also the home of a hard-hit member of the aristocracy who had sensibly conceived of it as a means of educating her five children and making sufficient money to maintain the fabric of her house. Alas, her idea came too late for the spores of dry rot had entered the soul of the place and the battle to exorcise them was already lost. But despite the duck boards in the attics and areas of brittle floor roped off for safety there was nothing shaky about the school. The Lady gave her charges good plain food and the education was in the hands of dedicated teachers. She, like Joan, despised retrenchment. The atmosphere was that of the country house, calm, cool and leisurely. There were horses to ride, grounds to explore and the kind of young friends we wanted Heather to have. Being the make of woman she was, and with her circumstances, the Lady was understanding of the new poor and the contradictions of life under Trust. Even so, we were the least opulent of all the school parents. The Lady's social position had attracted the attention of a few well-fed, triumphant field marshals of industry, and it was on occasion shaming to arrive at the school on Bizarro and park its battered frame beside some Silver Ghost or similar mobile testament to the commercial dream come true.

The Lady had a brother, a certain Lord Malcolm, and this man had found time in a life of robust activity to turn his eyes on Westminster. In the early Spring of that same year the Labour Government which had landslid to power in 1945 was due to be put to the vote and those of us who had money to win or no more money to lose were sick of being grey cats in the dark of a Socialist administration. Lord Malcolm became the Unionist Candidate for Inverness-shire. He was a bold, handsome man, who spoke with conviction and did not shrink from heckling. In the whole far-flung constituency which at that time included the Hebridean islands, he had no more fervent supporters than the Wilshins and the Freres.

The duties of a committee member of a local branch are varied. In the early days of the campaign a fighting fund is built up through the proceeds of coffee mornings and raffles, and envelopes have to be addressed, but when the testing day grows near these unheroic but necessary activities are put aside and the canvassers go forth in all their crusading strength. Joan bicycled here and there and in every house she entered she proclaimed the aims of Conservatism flatly and would not brook dispute. She had already gained the confidence of our friends on the railway by agitating for an improvement in their sanitation and had pressed successfully for a village refuse collection. This upset a few people who saw an addition of a few pence on the Rates as a poor exchange for ubiquitous dumping, but by showing that she, a loudly self-proclaimed Conservative, was concerned for the problems of those who voted otherwise, she did much to advance Lord Malcolm's support. Obversely she was impatient with those who, knowing the Right, failed to go out and preach it.

She considered me to be one of these. One day she said to me: 'We've got a job for you. As soon as you've put that together you must go to Dulnain Bridge to see a voter.'

'That' was a dissected Bizarro which was undergoing its Spring overhaul. Its parts were spread over a wide area which included the kitchen sink and a warm place on top of the Rayburn. The chickens required so little attention that I had found time to work on my machine. I was, until I received this instruction, perfectly happy.

'Must I?' In those days I was a shy young man, adverse to fresh human contact. I had tried to make it clear that I would do everything but canvass.

'You must. This woman seems to be a bit of a recluse, she lives in a place where Shiela can't possibly get her car. We tried yesterday. By her name we think she must be one of us so she won't need converting but we must offer a lift to the Polling Station. Every vote is going to count in this election', she added with religious fervour.

That was true, I knew, and I didn't mind making a simple offer. 'Right,' I said, screwing up a back brake, 'give me a couple of hours. Where is it? And what's her name?'

'Her house is called Poll Dubh and it's up on the moors behind that old castle. Her name is Marie D'Agincourt.'

'D'Agincourt? It's not possible! What, like the battle?'

'It seems so. That's how it's spelt on the electoral roll.'

'An extraordinary thing. My curiosity is growing.'

'Keep it growing then and get this thing out of here. Oh, my God', she added picking up an oily rag, 'is this one of my clean dish cloths?'

It was difficult to find Poll Dubh. Twice I turned off the main road and bucked my way along corrugated tracks of frozen mud in search of houses which vanished mirage-like as I drew near. As Bizarro vaulted along like a Spring lamb I took time to consider how hard is the task of the rural canvasser in these areas. Not only are the houses far-flung and widely spaced but their occupants are seldom known by the names which appear in the official lists. In order to distinguish Kenneth Mackenzie, the poacher, from Kenneth Mackenzie, the fencer, and both of them from Kenneth Mackenzie who sells coal, pseudonyms have been applied and directions are easily obtained to Kennie Salmon, Kennie the Stob, or Kennie Coal but it is often impossible to relate one to the other, especially when they live on the same moor.

Well, there wouldn't be many D'Agincourts around, of that I was sure, but the whereabouts of Poll Dubh continued to perplex me. I had a map and every so often stopped to refer to it. Poll Dubh was there, a small oblong at the end of a dotted line but I was in a valley between low hills which offered no significant landmark. Seeing a navigable slope I turned off the track and roared up thin heather. Bizarro was a good scrambler and took the naked hillside in its stride. From the crown of the ridge I saw indubitably what I had come to find.

It wasn't what I had expected. To live here at all the lady must have fallen upon hard times or have been incorrigibly eccentric, but I had envisaged a tidy little retreat, white-washed, with a few flowers growing and a neatly trimmed rowan tree entwined around a gaily painted front door. I am, at heart, an incurable romantic. But Poll Dubh was quite otherwise. A filthy hovel under a scabby roof of tin, it cringed in its own dark hollow beneath a ring of stunted birch. The front door, what was left of it, was held erect by a piece of rusty bed girder; small, mean windows were cracked in a dozen places; the walls, stained green and yellow with damp, had settled leaving a nasty fissure up the middle, and from the pot-less chimney stack a thin curl of vapour affronted the air with the stench of paraffin. The forecourt was a rippled sea of frost-warped mud.

I set Bizarro on its stand and advanced across the hardened morass. A few trapped tins gaped up at me, warning that I should watch my step. I reached the door and tapped carefully upon it. At least, I thought, there's someone here who may direct me, refusing to believe this was the house of D'Agincourt. Following my tap there was a short silence, then a shuffling noise and the wood creaked open a dozen suspicious inches. An ugly and belligerent face glared through the crack.

'Bugger off!' it said, meaning it.

Taken somewhat aback, I was still able to hear my wife's voice, 'Every vote is going to count . . .' Though this creature was certainly not she whom I sought it was as much entitled to express a political preference as any other in the land. If it had no such preference here was my chance to give it one.

'Excuse me,' I said, recoiling from a foetid stench which stormed through the door, 'I'm here on behalf of the Unionist Party. Let me tell you what we stand for. I'm sure you'll agree we've had more than enough of this socialism.'

'Bugger off,' repeated the crone, brushing some cobwebs away with a crooked hand, 'or I'll pu' ma dog on yer.' This was no idle threat for I had noticed a large hound of mixed parentage licking its jaws in the shadows. I stepped back, checked but not defeated, and stated firmly: 'I'm for Lord Malcolm.' To confirm my credentials I held up a poster which showed the candidate's handsome face. The firm jaw, clear eyes and general air of transparent honesty coupled with a modest yet confident glance which seemed to embrace a brave new Britain, had been known to break down many a socialist wife and put her at odds with her husband. The magic had not lost its power. 'Com ben the hoose', she said. 'I wouldn'a open ma door to yon other bugger, talkin' aboot Krupps an' Hutler.' What! I thought, surely the echoes of victory haven't taken five years to reach this place! Then I understood. 'Oh no indeed. We've no time for Cripps and Attlee, we're on the other side. We're going to change the government. But I won't come in, only we'd like to offer you a lift to Carr Bridge on Polling Day so that you can make your cross for Lord Malcolm. If you'd be at the main road at noon on the twenty-third, there'll be a car waiting. Now, I wonder if you would help me? I'm looking for a Mrs Marie . . .'

She interrupted me fiercely. 'Aye, I'll tak' a luft wi' yer, and mak' a puckle crosses if it'll help send them buggers doon the road. Wasn'a for that lot Dargancort'd still be in me bed o'nights. Spent ma bloody time cuttin' timber for 'em in the war, he used to say, and yer still canny get a decent fill for ya belly. Starved, 'e was, wi' the rationing, and 'e buggered off back to Newfunlan a twelve month Wednesday first.'

I tried to keep my face straight. 'You'll be Mrs D'Agincourt!' I said, aware that my quest was ended. A dottle she may have been but she did not miss the amazement in my voice. 'Aye, ut's a loony name, an't it?' she remarked. 'Ma man haad it fra folks wha' braat 'im up in Newfunland, aye in the Laabrador. Frenchies they were, 'e said.' She regarded me sternly through keen little eyes which looked like diamonds set in brown peat: 'Now mind ya dinny forget the car on t' day. I'll put them buggers off doon the road yet.'

It was an exciting election night. These were the days before computers presupposed the outcome and late the next morning the issue was still in doubt. At last we realised with sinking hearts that 'Krupps and Hutler' were going to hang on, though only by the skin of their teeth. We went to bed in the grey daylight, disappointed but resigned, knowing that we had done our best. And when, two days later, Lord Malcolm was triumphantly proclaimed the Member from the Town Hall in Inverness, a Caesar crowned, we knew that our best and that of Marie D'Agincourt with many others, had not been bad at all.

A month later, eight weeks to the day from their arrival at the station the young chickens were ready for market. A man came from Aberdeen, gave us some money and took them away in his van. Ninety-two birds had survived. They had eaten less than we had expected and the profit margin was good. Reading this as a sure pointer to expansion we bought two more brooders and since I had recently had the good fortune to come across a farmer who had given up poultry in favour of pigs, the feeding prospects were good. This man still had half a ton of mash in his barn which he was happy to sell me for what it had cost him. It was the best of omens.

In any branch of animal production the soft-hearted should guard against emotional involvement with his product. When our first batch of chickens went we were quite cast down. Our only comfort was contained in the sentiment that sustains a court in mourning: 'The chickens are dead, long live the chickens', and indeed no sooner were the brooders empty than they were replenished with a fresh intake. It was, of course, a collective affection we felt, for chickens don't usually have much individuality. Yet in the first batch Joan had remarked upon a tiny bird, a black feathered body amid a host of brown, which seemed to lead a solitary life. It ate in its own time and would often stand alone in the same corner of the brooder. This independent chick soon began to exhibit features that implied the most basic of differences and when at the age of six weeks its small head remained pale amid a host of reddening combs we knew that a sexer must have blundered. We had a hen. 'A hundred men and a girl, or nearly,' said Joan, 'this one's not going anywhere.' She christened it Blackie and it became her firm friend.

We produced poussin successfully for six months and when the operation had to halt it was through no fault of ours. The market, as Jim had warned, simply dried up. When he came for the last time our retailer said: 'I'll not be back meantime. There's too many at it. But when I want some more I'll be in touch.'

From our point of view this was not quite conclusive. There were, at that very moment, two hundred day-olds chirping at the station. Since we couldn't send them back we would have to make the best of them. We had plenty of food and ample accommodation but in the absence of a commercial outlet we were going to have a multitude of pets!

Bob, who believed in simple rationalising, came up with a suggestion. Why not grow the birds on to maturity? There were local fishmongers and he knew them all. (Under Kennie Salmon he had served an adventurous apprenticeship.) They would be anxious to buy fat birds in the tourist season. It was an excellent idea and to start with it worked out well: had we had the space for it the thing would have been a winner.

We continued to buy day-olds, though on a reduced scale. After eight weeks they all lived in the mushroom house but it soon became full. Some had to grow up in the Bungalow and in effect to share our bed and board. Joan, never long suffering, soon became affronted by the stench. It was pretty bitter and she maintained stoutly that we should all be poisoned. On the other hand young Richard, her primary concern in that context, was fascinated by the birds and spent many an hour closely observing life in the brooders. I was then well into that state of monomania which I cannot help substituting for a balanced interest and had begun to see myself as a notable figure in the world of poultry husbandry; so my son's interest was heartening. 'Perhaps he's going to be a poultryman too', I remarked to Joan but she shook her head vigorously. 'You should ask Mrs Leslie about that, she has other plans for him.'

In having loyal and versatile Bob to attend our every need, and that gratis, we were blessed. Yet Fate, chary of kind offerings in other ways, now saw fit to make another award. It came in the person of Mrs Leslie, the wife of a railway ganger, who lived in the cottages opposite. This woman, the mother of an impeccably groomed six-year-old boy, loved children with an uncritical ardour. Richard, our son, brown, curly headed and with a deceptively angelic look of sunlight soap and new mown hay had long been the subject of her unstinted admiration. One summer's morning, as she watched him pelting a shrinking hen with lumps of mushroom compost, she could stand it no longer. 'Mrs Frere,' she said, marching up to Joan who was sunning herself on our steps, 'I want to look after your son. I think he is a most beautiful boy. I am qualified to be his nanny as that was my job before I married. *Please* let me help you with him, I know you are a very busy person.'

Joan went a little pale beneath her tan. I know how she must have felt – I'd had the same sort of thoughts when Bob had proposed himself. She hesitated while the spectre of wages rose before her, clanking its chains dismally. Mrs Leslie misinterpreted the cause of her unease. 'I *am* a qualified person,' she repeated desperately, 'Truly I am. My last position was with Lord and Lady Winbush and I *only* left because Viscount Robin went away to boarding school. It almost broke my heart. But look,' she added, taking a well worn postcard from her apron, 'the little darling hasn't forgotten me.' Joan looked at the image of a smiling young man in an Eton collar. On the back, scrawled in an aristocratically careless hand, were the words: 'To dear old LES. Having a smashing time here. Cheers, love and all the best, from Robbie Gorse.' 'I've full references too, of course', added Mrs Leslie persuasively.

Joan didn't doubt that she was in the presence of a professional. That was the cause of her greatest embarrassment. Weak with it, and lost for words, she subsided on the steps. The new nanny said: 'Mrs Frere, you're exhausted. I will start at once. It's a fine day for drying and I'm sure there's some washing to be done. All this is a great deal too much for you: cooking, cleaning, gardening and looking after the wee man. You'll wear your fingers to the bone!'

'Wear my fingers to the bone,' repeated Joan stupidly, and gave in to the inevitable.

Mrs Leslie enveloped Richard at once and spent more time with us than she did at the cottage on the railway. Joe Leslie who had spent his life on the permanent way acknowledged his wife's burning need to have a younger child to care for. A dark, dour man, as solid as the chocks he drove between chair and rail, he seemed the direct contrast to the cheerful ardent woman who had travelled widely with her families and had acquired their ways and speech. Yet they were a vastly contented couple. At the Bungalow Mrs Leslie's self-imposed duties were not limited to the care of her 'wee man' and she capably tackled every domestic task which came along. As Joan remarked in Irish style: 'Bob does everything and Mrs Leslie does the rest', and the fact that the only insult we could ever offer either of them was the mention of wages filled our cup of happiness to the brim.

The nanny was convinced that her new charge, when grown to man's estate, would go into the Navy. It arose, one can only imagine, when she saw him bombarding an empty baked bean tin with stones until it sank in the former straw-soaking tank which was by then half filled with green slime. On the other hand, it might have been his lovable habit of treating her with a kind of autocratic contempt which she saw as a fitting quality for the assumption of high rank. 'He will be an admiral', she stated flatly and from this prophecy nothing would move her. One day, in sardonic mood, I tried to convince her that other members of my family occasionally made a shambles and that this congenital peculiarity was best limited in the opportunities given to it. It began when she enquired about Sir Bartle.

He hung, at this time, on a smooth face of wall above the lavatory pan. It was the best we could do for him in the circumstances though we regretted the insult to a man who had been in his time a great administrator and holder of high office. I explained to Mrs Leslie that on the whole our family had been a harmless bunch of landed rustics who lived well on the substances of the heiresses they invariably married. Harmless, at least when they ran their small estates but the few individuals who came out of the comfortable rut tended to be destructive. 'The present lavatory attendant', I said, 'did well until he became a Member of the Council of India but in 1874 he signed the private minute that produced the Afghan war. He was, so they say, thrawn and smug, unable to doubt the morality of any course that he himself recommended. I'm a bit like that too.'

'A great gentleman', claimed Mrs Leslie, 'but you said something about an admiral, like my wee man is going to be.'

'An admiral is it?' I mused, 'well we had one of those too. That's what's worrying me. He nearly sank a flag-ship.'

'Oh no!' Mrs Leslie was thrilled. 'One of theirs? In the First War?'

'Well actually it was one of ours and in peace time. It wasn't really his fault though he does appear to have been a bit unbending. He was captain of the battle cruiser *Renown* and was involved in a naval exercise with, among others, the battleship *Hood*. They collided. It seems to have been a case of perfect discipline taking precedence over ordinary common sense. Like in that Balaclava business. The order was to turn in towards each other, and turn in they did: and went on with it even when it was obvious to the youngest cabin boy that they were going to bump. No one was drowned but it cost the tax payer a bit of money. My cousin was lightly censured and instantly promoted to Rear

Admiral. But it was his last appointment. Well, nearly his last.'

'He rose higher?'

'Depends on the viewpoint. He was, in due course, promoted to the rank of Richard's godfather.'

The whole recital had lifted Mrs Leslie to the seventh heaven of delight. It pleased us too for it was good to recall the days when our family had been rich and powerful. She made us tea and we charged our cups to the memory of heroic deeds.

Down at the straw wash Richard had just discharged a salvo of stones and mud at a raft which carried the toy survivors of some fancied engagement. It tipped over into the slime and all hands were lost.

As the weeks went by our birds became very big and for every pound they gained they seemed to need twice as much food. Soon we had a feeding, as well as an accommodation, problem. We invested in a huge cast-iron boiler in which we cooked potatoes by the bag and my farmer friend, who had now given up pigs, was pleased to offer me his supply of fish meal. We spoke of getting a goat for milk and no sooner had this been resolved than a goat turned up unheralded. A wanderer by nature, she had proved a problem to the owners who were glad to part with her and we saw her as the answer to a diet deficiency in our stock until we found that she was barren. By then she had become a pet so her position in the household was secure. Her needs were small: a diet of old shoes, stale bread, potato scraps and the occasional bowl of bran sufficed her and in return she performed the office of court jester. When things went wrong there was always Katy to divert us.

Soon we needed diverting. The overcrowded conditions in the mushroom house brought on a wave of cannibalism and once the birds had tasted the blood of their fellows it was most difficult to control. We lost many cocks in an orgy of fratricide and it became encumbent upon us to eat them. As it had been with the mushrooms so it now was with the white meat of the fowl. Delicacy was demoted to standard diet, the cry was 'Chicken with everything!'

To curb the birds' savagery we pared and blunted the beaks, a hundred at a time. We were watching our profits eating themselves away. The plain truth was that we simply didn't have room for the numbers: the birds' quarters were bulging and soon, in common humanity, we allowed them to overflow and seek a tiny measure of free range in the garden. Here they scratched, and pecked and voided until our carefully tended grass became mottled with their droppings and the air was made hideous with their incessant adolescent squawking.

When the first batch was twenty weeks old we sold them to a local fishmonger. It was a relief rather than a triumph to see them go. We had resolved to have no more day-olds, we wanted to phase the business out but we still had several hundred in various stages of growth. And just then from out of the blue came an offer that it was hard to refuse. A large hotel in the area was about to give a major function: poultry was in short supply at the time and somehow they had heard that we might supply their needs. They wanted sixty tender cocks, young, fat, dead and roughly plucked and they wanted them at once. In a sellers' market they proposed an excellent price, more than twice what we were getting. There was one snag and that a weighty one: neither of us had ever pulled a bird's neck, nor had the stomach for it, and Bob who would have done it was in bed with a bad attack of 'flu.

My first instinct was to turn down the offer. I was sure that I could never bring myself to execute a bird. As individuals I liked them, fed them, tended them in sickness and spoke to them in my whimsical way. They trusted me. I was not unaware of the flawed morality of my aversion but it was no comfort. To pay an assassin is one thing, to do the act oneself is quite another. But I still had lingering ambitions to be a proper poultryman and to attain this end I would have to put aside my squeamishness.

I resolved I would do it in the morning. That night I

moved sixty birds into an empty compound and withheld their food. They regarded me, one hundred and twenty small bright eyes, each with a question in it. It was horrible. How could I be sure that they did not read my thoughts? Suppressing a sudden urge to fill the feeding bowls and cry 'You are reprieved!' I ran from the mushroom house.

In the morning it was worse, much worse. Now the moment was at hand I was physically unequal to it. I groped dazedly for the brown body of a fat cockerel and snatching it to my chest, took it by the legs and slipped my fingers round its narrow neck. It was so thin, so small, so vulnerable and as the bird felt my nervousness its tiny pulse began to beat like a drum. I could not do it: this common-place act which any farmer's wife would treat as a routine duty was beyond me. Before my eyes there was another picture, and it was that of myself held by the ankles in a giant's hand, awaiting the clutch and snap which would send me into Eternity. At the sheer horror of the image my uncoordinated muscles snatched and something gave inside the neck. There was a great leap of nerve and I lost my grip. The thing fell to the floor, thrashing wildly, regained its feet and did a brief tottering dance while its head rotated like a bolas stone on the string of its elongated neck. It rushed into a corner of the room as though even in its latest moment it might find some safety there, fell over, twitched once and became a decently dead bird.

I killed them all that morning, robbed each little con-sciousness of its light and whatever joy it had in living. It is idle to deny that with each succeeding cockerel it was easier for me and less painful for them: but I hated it no less, and resolved never to repeat it.

The tending of our deep litter hens, conceived only as a sideline, gave more pleasure and profit than the main pro-ject. After the blood and guts of cannibalism, the stench of overcrowded quarters and the final trauma of mass execu-tion it was an idyll. We housed fifty Exchequer Leghorns, a breed of pretty birds, in the garage whose doors had been exchanged for the panels of vita glass discarded from the

Bungalow. They had space, light, fresh air and the chemical heat beneath them produced through the action of their own droppings in deep straw. Coming as point-of-lay pullets in November we cherished them and they did us proud. In order to offer them the maximum of laying time I had constructed a gadget to give them artificial light. It looked like a time bomb, its chief component being an alarm clock with sawn off hands which made and broke an electric current, and each morning at six and each evening at four it would switch on a number of strong bulbs and turn them off three hours later.

Yes, we enjoyed our hens: they were the best part of the time we spent in poultry. It was easy to share the birds' contentment when we knew that we should never be called upon to kill them. We went on rearing cockerels for live collection in small batches for we had become very conscious of their need for space. For the Christmas market we bought two dozen turkey poults but with so small a quantity we were faced again with the problem of emotional involvement. We knew each turkey by name and by habit and when the time came to give them to our butcher we were uneasy at his suggestion, kindly meant, to let us have one back, dressed ready for the table, for our own consumption. We proposed instead that he should take all twenty-four of our birds and give us, if he would, a member of some other family. He smilingly agreed but in the event it was impossible to know if he had honoured the promise. It had to be taken on trust, as one takes the residue of a loved one in the tiny urn, because all ashes and all dressed poultry look exactly alike.

It was a good Christmas for us, thanks to our small successes, and since the new year is a time for resolutions we decided to move into ducks. We would try a hundred Aylesbury day-olds for such seemed exactly right for our situation. We had the meal and potatoes to fatten them, could run them in unrestricted woodland, make cheap shelters against the weather, be free of most diseases and the fear of cannibalism and they were to go away live by train when ready to a Perthshire distributor who had proposed an excellent price.

We found the chicks were charming little chaps, fluffy and yellow, with bold appetites and a strong will to survive. From the first batch we took the strongest and best looking, put a ring on his leg, and called him Champion. This act was part of a tradition which had started with Blackie, Joan's personal hen. We had continued it in the selection of a monster Rhode Island cockerel, from the second batch, a brute of a bird called Hannibal. In his time he had conducted a reign of terror in the mushroom house, being a skilled practitioner in the art of evisceration, but then Joan had given Blackie to him in marriage and they lived placidly together in a grace and favour hencoop in the wood.

The ducklings grew like magic. At the end of a month they were of even size and we had not lost a single one. The time, once again, had come to be bold. We ordered five hundred more. The first batch was ten weeks old when they went, fat as butter balls, on the train and the cheque which came back was equally fat. From the second, much larger batch, we removed a chance female, called her Mato, and hinted to a bright-eyed Champion that when she grew up she would be his woman.

Although the forest was many acres in extent the Aylesburys made limited use of it. They preferred to congregate behind our boundary fence, making the ground foul with their droppings, and if they found a weak point they would pour through it onto the fresh grass of the lawn. One June night we came back from Grantown to find that several hundred birds had invaded our territory. Bob and Richard, who helped us to drive them back, swore that they had known nothing of the invasion. There had been a 'dorg rough' session that evening which had fully occupied them. It was well after midnight when the last wagging tail was pushed through the hole in the fence and even then the ducks' day was not quite over. We went to bed by the soft light of the afterglow, that fleeting moment in the northern mid-summer night when sunset and sunrise fuse, and no sooner was Joan between the sheets than she cried out: 'My God, there's something in here.' 'Of course there is', I said, squeezing in beside her, 'and it's me. What more could you possibly ask?' At that moment my feet reached a bundle of warm feathers. 'Ouch!' I squawked, as loudly as the duck, and sprang back onto the floor where I trod on another one. All at once the room was loud with quacking; the birds were everywhere. Brushing them aside I reached the light switch. Two Aylesburys, half asleep, fell off the top of the hanging wardrobe and thudded to the floor. By then Joan was at the door. 'I'll get these devils up', she cried, cheerfully hysterical, 'they've done this! I wondered why Richard was smirking – Bob! Come here at once.' She pulled on a dressing gown. 'No, you get them. Make them take these birds away.' I hastened to obey but as I went through the dark 'den' I fell over a recumbent Katy who had recently taken to sleeping there. It was the second time in twenty four hours that she had tried to kill me for earlier, as I had turned into our gate from the station road on the motorcycle, she had pulled her grazing chain tight and caught me round the neck.

But such things as ducks in the bedchamber and strangulation by goat chains were minor irritations in a general run of good luck. At last it seemed that we were on the road to riches and in the *hubris* which clouded my head I failed to take more than passing note of the large amount of blood which was appearing in the birds' droppings.

We did not know it then but the next, and largest consignment, was to be our last. So numerous were the birds ready for market that we did not have sufficient crates for them and we hastily packed a few in large cardboard boxes liberally punched with air holes. One of these makeshift containers collapsed on the platform and a dozen fat ducks flapped down onto the railway line. The south train was only a few minutes away. While Joan held the box Bob and I ran about on the tracks trying to catch the awkward birds and restore them to the platform. It was not an easy task.

They fluttered about in blissful ignorance of the big locomotive as it rapidly bore down upon them. Thank God, we
had a friend at court. Willie Calder saw the situation from
his signal box and halted the train a hundred yards from the
station. As he was to tell us later, from where he stood the
birds were invisible but he could make out Bob and me
doing a jig on the railway line while Joan seemed to hold
out imploring hands in an attempt to dissuade us from an
act of joint suicide. A witness to the red carpet incident, as
well as other weird performances, he had every reason to
suspect lapses of sanity on the part of his unpredictable
neighbours.

I must now be brief. This is another cartload of rocks
from Mount Pelion. By next morning seventy ducks, two
weeks from maturity, had died. Others followed in quick
succession and by mid-day we had obtained an opinion
from a Veterinary College in Edinburgh. It was bleak. Our
flock was infected with a genus of bacteria known as the
Salmonella. Since they ran together on foul ground it was
unlikely that any bird would escape infection and our
informant made it clear that on no account must they be
eaten. It could be dangerous, he said, implying sudden
death, for he could not discount a connection with the
bacillus Botulinus. 'Cremate the dead', he ended shortly as
though out of patience with those who had created their
own bubonic plague, 'and burn the shelters. I am sorry,
there is nothing else to be done.'

Lucky ducks died quickly, as if felled by heart attack, but
others lingered on with anal sphincters voiding green slime;
and some, including Champion, a mere two score, survived
the pestilence. We burned the bodies on an enormous pyre
set off by petrol and splintered wood from the shelters. The
air was filled with the smell of roast duckling and a thick
grey smoke drifted among the forest trees. Bob and I
walked sadly back to the Bungalow to find Joan tending
something in a box. It was Champion, clean, dry with deep
straw around him and food within reach of his bill. 'I'll keep
him in here at night', said Joan, 'and he can go for a walk on

clean grass – if there's such a thing left.' Champion, half asleep, nodded his head up and down like a little white magistrate in his ermine.

Joan needn't have worried. Champion was not destined for burning. Instead he drowned two days later in the potato boiler which she had filled with clean water so that he could get some swimming. He was buried, decently, in a grave. And that, most certainly, was that.

The Ministry of National Insurance sent me a pettish letter saying that I hadn't stamped my card for three years. I couldn't deny it and the rebuke pointed me firmly to a decision I had already half made. I would give up my attempts at business! 'Bob', I said, 'for Heaven's sake find me a job. I know you don't think it's right for me to work, except on my own account, but needs must when the devil drives. There must be something – you know the chaps – felling trees, digging drains, planting, anything.'

Bob mused, in deep disapproval. At last he muttered 'Planting?'

'Yes, why not? Surely I could learn to do it?'

'It's no' right, it's no' fitting. What'll Mistress Frere say about it?' He alone held on to the social pretences which the situation had long outgrown.

'I don't suppose she'll be overjoyed, but what else can we do? Don't forget I used to work at Glenmore Lodge with Mr Randall.'

'Ah but that wasn'a where ye lived. Folks know ye here.'

'Well, we won't be here much longer unless I do something. The Insurance people want to take me to court. And others. Come on, let's go and see Kenny Stob. It's high time I found some other beggar to stamp my cards.'

8 ❧ *Social Occasions*

My return to the ranks of the gainfully employed took place on a wet November morning. At six, when Bob brought our morning tea, it was raining darkly through a thick mist and the pines were moping in the forest. 'Oh no', muttered Joan in great petulance, 'take it away, Bob. I can't drink tea at this hour.' My own response to this rude awakening was not enthusiastic. It is easy for me to get up at any time but, while I can be brisk and gay in the small hours if a day in the mountains is to follow, my spirits wilt at the prospect of routine occasions. Bob, true to his promise, had spoken to Kenny Stob, and we were now contracted to perform a five and a half day week of fifty-three hours planting trees for the princely sum of six pounds less income tax and national insurance contributions. It had been hinted also that overtime might be available though how this could be fitted in, at least during the dark winter days, was more than I could imagine.

We stuffed ourselves with brose, scrambled egg and fried potato, all of which were related to our recent ill-starred project. We shared the oat meal with the Leghorns who gave us the eggs and we still had two tons of potatoes. Only our stock of fishmeal was redundant. Even Joan, the ever inventive cook, could not incorporate that in our diet. Having eaten, and washed it away with tea, we marched out into the dripping world upon which the early light had so far made no impression whatsoever.

The job had one merit: it was near at hand. Twenty minutes later we stood, with half a dozen bedraggled and yawning others, on the edge of the moor which was to be planted. The Stob, who would give us our orders for the day, was late. By the time his van drew up at a gate, we had lost half an hour's twilight but as Bob pointed out to me the Stob would still expect us to plant the same number of trees in the time remaining.

We gathered round our employer. He had a tall figure, buckled forward at the top end, and a whisky face: even in the half light you could sense his nose aglow. An expatriate Aberdonian he spoke in a rich but quite unintelligible dialect and it was as well for me that his instructions were brief, simple and supported by expressive mime. When my turn came he thrust a planting spade, a thing like a lawn trimmer, into my hand and looped over my shoulder a haversack containing twelve hundred tiny trees of the species Pinus sylvestris. I gathered, not at once, that all of them must be firmly planted by five-thirty or I should not need to come back the next day.

By the time the instruction was finished there were some tattered rents in the eastern sky and a sickly sun was convalescing behind them. We took up our positions about a yard apart, with spades at the ready. In unison we drove our spades into the heather, withdrew them, reinserted at right angles, lifted the flap of turf thus formed, stuck in a tree and trod down the ground with our feet. It was like bayonetting the helpless body of the moor. We took a single long stride forward and repeated the process.

I mastered it only slowly. I fumbled with my plants and they fell on the ground but the corporate movement of the squad made it impossible to reverse mistakes. Many of my trees, if they survived, were destined for horizontal growth while others, inserted crown down, might only succeed in New Zealand. We went on marching across the squelching moor as daylight grew in a yellow haze and the rain came down in buckets.

At ten o'clock a halt was allowed for ten minutes. Crouching together, the workers drank tea from their thermos flasks while the Stob drew a half bottle from his planting bag and gulped down a few mouthfuls of whisky. I was distressed to find that while the bags of my companions looked thin mine still bulged with trees. One of the planters, a baby-faced man called Sma' Pim had noticed my cumbersome attempts to insert plants into their flaps and saw fit to offer some worldly advice. Glancing over his shoulder to ensure that the Stob was out of sight he drew me aside: 'No' laak thaat, dinny tak' a' that sweat aboot it, ye'll nae get a medal. See this.' He slammed in his spade twice. Here the ground was soft peat and untypical: it was mostly hard shingle which jarred the wrists and made a deep incision hard to come by. 'Easy groun', we put a puckle here' said the villain Pim as he seized a handful of trees and consigned them en masse to earth, 'yon'll mak up for them ye can't get doon in the harrd.' He gave me a darkly fetching grin. 'In guid groun' ye can sink a reet bagful and no bugger'll be the wiser.' Though seriously doubting the morality of the suggestion it obviously improved my performance.

We persisted in our job. The winter days grew shorter, darker and more dreary: soon the moor was grey with wet snow. Joan, left alone with Richard through all the daylight hours, became a little depressed. Therefore I was delighted when she said to me one evening:

'Arabella's coming to stay.'

'Arabella? Oh that's great. For how long?'

'Indefinite duration. She hasn't any plans.'

Arabella, until recently, had been receptionist at her aunt's hotel in Grantown. Now the aunt had died, the hotel was for sale and Arabella was at a loose end. She was a rather splendid-looking woman. A natural male interest in the idea was partially eclipsed by the dismal need for economy. I remarked, looking mean: 'Indefinite? Won't that be rather . . .'

'Expensive for us', Joan supplied. 'No, it won't. She's coming as a paying guest.'

This sounded an excellent idea. Joan got on well with Arabella who was bright and fashionable. They would amuse each other, our slender economy would be stimulated and there would be two attractive women in the house for the price of one. As a person who always sees temporary expedient in the light of ultimate salvation I was quite beside myself with satisfaction. Arabella duly arrived and very soon thereafter she and I were involved in a mild flirtation which was so light-hearted and innocent that

Joan didn't seem to mind it at all. One evening we heard of Edward, a rising young accountant, who wanted badly to marry Arabella. Joan could not wait to invite Edward for the weekend.

It was easy to like Edward. He was conscientious, serious and progressive but in contrast to these dull qualities – any one of which I might have possessed to advantage – he could be light-hearted and amusing, and he was always generous. He was quite besotted with Arabella but she, not long widowed, wanted to be sure of her feelings before she married again. She asked our advice and we dissected Edward with surgical precision but when he was put together again it was impossible to deny his eligibility. We said so but Arabella still demurred. 'The trouble is', she said, 'he's too short.' She turned musing eyes in my direction: 'I love tall men, like Richard.' Joan smiled, more or less to herself, and I said hastily: 'Nonsense – you make him sound like a dwarf. Edward's of middle height and well proportioned. And anyway', I added, 'I'm not six feet.'

'Oh, you must be', she breathed, straight out of *Woman's Own*.

'I'm not.' It is, in fact, one of my minor regrets that I never quite made two yards. I won't now. I might have done so had I not laden myself with enormously heavy iron weights during my growing period. At fifteen, recovering from an ear operation, I had been the archetype weed in the Charles Atlas advertisement but had then been introduced to weight-lifting. On the whole I have never had cause to regret it: a strongly muscled body is a joy to use even though an extreme feeling of well-being tends to make people indolent in other ways. How many millionaires are perfect physical specimens, may I ask?

Edward spent several weekends with us. He took us around the country in his car and seemed determined that we should enjoy ourselves at his expense. Arabella was giving him rather a cold shoulder but he stiffened a dog-like devotion to her with dignity and was never lachrymose. He was, and no doubt still is, a man of quite unnatural calmness and so self-effacing that in certain circumstances he became almost invisible.

One day he invited the three of us to drive with him to Loch Ness where John Cobb in his jet boat *Crusader* was practising for an attempt on the world water speed record. We parked on a high point of the road and watched *Crusader* skimming across the mirror-like surface of the loch at enormous speed. As a spectacle it was almost too exciting; we sweated with fear for this brave man in his contest with such unknown forces and would have turned away from the sight in horror had we known that three days later Cobb, tossed into the air by an iron-hard ripple, was to die at his very moment of triumph. Later I was depressed at the thought of my own dull life and the loss of opportunities that might have led to fame. I had a burning need to exert myself, to do something dramatic, and when Edward thoughtfully suggested that I might like to drive his car for the rest of the journey I accepted at once. We had drained a few jugs of beer at an hotel by the loch and were in sparkling merry form.

With Arabella beside me in the front seat I was compelled to exhibit my driving skills. It had been, in fact, a long time since I had driven a car but it is an ability, like swimming, skating and making love, which once learnt is never quite forgotten. What I had lost in refinement I had gained in panache. 'Oh, you are a wonderful driver, Richard', Arabella murmured, eyes moist with passion or the wind, as I hurled Edward's family saloon round blind corners and truculently overhauled big lorries on the hills.

After passing through Inverness I wearied of the main road and proposed using a small hill track as a long cut back to Carr Bridge. I have never rallied but the idea appeals to me. By then Edward's car had become a part of my mood and it twisted uncomplainingly up the tight bends above the Nairn valley, spurting gravel from its churning wheels. Conversation had lapsed and the only sound in the car, apart from the grinding shock of overstressed machinery, was my loud hummed rendering of

Wagner's 'Ride of the Valkyries'. In this heroic vacuum I
felt the exciting touch of Arabella's hand on my arm, mis-
took the reason for it, gave her a warm look and promptly
ran into a wall. There was a loud crunch. 'Oh God', I said,
falling back to earth.

The offside wing of Edward's car was like a cauliflower
fashioned in tin and the headlamp resembled an eye which
has been flipped from its socket. 'You damn fool', said Joan
smartly, 'you were driving like a madman. Showing off, as
usual.' I didn't relish the remark, made in front of Arabella,
but she, fond woman, countered with: 'He couldn't help it,
the road's so narrow here.' 'Rot! He was simply trying to
impress you', replied my wife, 'and seems to have done so.'
In that sharp rejoinder I saw the first wisp of a cloud settle
over my pleasant little ménage à trois.

While we contended thus Edward, whose loss it was, had
wandered away and could be seen examining a patch of
gorse as though it held some significance for him. Bewildered at first by this strange conduct I soon realised that it
was merely an expression of his extreme courtesy. Knowing
that I would, or should, feel remorse at my furious driving
he wanted to show that the partial ruin of his car was of no
real account. When I said how sorry I was and offered to
pay for the damage he waved my words aside. 'No need to
worry about it. Please don't! As long as it'll get us home –
that's the main thing. My insurance will pay up; I have
taken a super one.' He paused while he looked from me to
Arabella, then from her to Joan, and added, 'One should be
covered against all third party risks, I think.' Seeing a dark
look on my wife's face, a sure sign of a growing turmoil
within, I realised that in one matter at least he was very well
insured.

We had been planting trees for five months when an
absent cat came back to take up residence among the
pigeons. As Bob and I wended our weary way up to the
Bungalow on a bland March evening we were surprised to
see a trim grey sports car standing at the gate. Most of our
friends had feet, a few ran bicycles but callers in cars were

infrequent. I concluded with irritation that it must be Chambers, a young sadist from the Ministry of National Insurance. Since I had committed the heinous crime of Not Stamping my Cards he had pursued me with the zeal of a Javert. My proposal to him that I ought to opt out of the Health Service had been rejected, many times more than once, with bureaucratic scorn.

'Go in first,' I said to Bob, 'and make him go away. Say I've been crushed under a tree or something', but it was too late. Our approach had been observed from a window. All at once the front door flew open and a thick-set, familiar figure was revealed. 'Good God', I said, 'It's Randall! Where on earth did he get that car?' We met half way up the steps with a round of back-slapping and shouted greeting. 'Peter! This is Bob', I said, 'Our strength and comfort!' The two men shook hands but it was plain that they didn't take to one another. Had they been dogs they would have raised their hackles and urinated on adjacent trees.

The five of us sat round the teapot while Randall commandeered the conversation and brought us up to date with his affairs. It was a rake's progress. His father had set him up in a good business in Cardiff but he had steadily grown bored with it. Days spent on the Brecon Beacons merely served to remind him of the great hills of Scotland and, he added, the company of his friends. Twenty-four hours earlier he had reached breaking point, shut his office door, pinned a note upon it, and driven north with as many of his possessions as his car would carry and no word of explanation to anyone. 'Won't your parents be worried?' asked Joan, 'I think you should let them know what's happening. When will you be going back?'

'Never', stated Peter with a grin. 'My old man will square it up. I'm going to stay in the north now. I wondered – would you mind having me for a week while I make some plans?'

'Of course you must stay', she said, amazing me by her cordiality. Later, when I commented upon it, she explained: 'Do you good to have him around for a bit. You haven't

climbed for ages. All this mooning around with women isn't
a good thing.'

To do him justice Randall insisted on paying for his keep
but it soon became apparent that the self-appointed time
limit on his stay was no better than a careless jest and
nothing was ever said about it again. Of course I enjoyed
his company now that we were able to afford him. The
thing we had in common was so dear to my heart that it
blinded me, as it had before, to his self-seeking and pettish
attitudes. There was a disruptive element in his character
which made it impossible for him to accept any status quo,
and my planting job was anathema to him. 'Chaps like us
don't work for other people', he claimed, 'we do the
employing.' Though the wounds inflicted on my sense of
self-reliance were still raw I saw his uncritical faith as a sure
ointment which would mend them.

One of his many suggestions completely captured my
fancy. It was that we should start a climbing magazine. The
outlay would be small and there was no need to give up my
job. On a wave of enthusiasm we launched our project with
a number of letters to notable mountaineers. The response
was kindly and helpful. N.E. Odell, last man to see Mallory
and Irving on Everest's North Ridge, promised us an
article and reminded me – as though I needed reminding! –
of a day I had spent with him in the Cairngorms in 1938.
Others, equally famous, sent us best wishes for an original
project with a variety of contributions. So far so good: much
better than we had expected, but as soon as we began to
seek a sponsor or a publisher who would take the risk it was
a different story. All said no and only some took the trouble
to tell us why; briefly they doubted an adequate circulation
and wondered why we had not approached advertisers to
help with production costs. This we did, writing to manu-
facturers of climbing equipment, and we had some promising replies but there was still a gap between ways and means
– a chasm with which I had long been over-familiar. It was
plain that we must have some personal capital to put into
the scheme. This stark fact gave Randall the lever he wanted.

'You must finish with that planting ploy and join up with me. No more excuses. I've seen Mr Jackson of the Estate Office' (he had indeed made a mysterious trip to Grantown that morning) 'and he wants a fencing contractor. *I've* bought the tools but I can do nothing on my own. If you will stop sticking in trees for that stupid pittance we'll make real money at once and save it for the first issue of the magazine.'

I gave in, offered the Stob my notice and received in return some lying time (back money) and my insurance card. A small area of it only was concealed beneath attractively coloured stamps. I saw, with misgivings, it was due for renewal and wondered how I should clothe its naked parts. Chambers, still working on year three of my defection, would soon call again and be mighty disapproving of my latest move. Bob, too, when told of my decision had been taken aback. As he was a man who never spoke ill of anybody it came as a shock to hear him say: 'I dinna think Mr Randall'll be of much use to you. He'll just pull ye doon.'

'I'm sorry you feel that way about him, Bob. But you won't leave us?'

'No, I'll not do that. And I'll make my contribution just the same. I reckon you'll need it and Mistress Frere will want me around onyways.'

Throughout the next month Peter and I built our first fence. It was pleasant piece work and by using all the daylight hours we made some money. After paying into the float we took out a wage which varied according to the week's performance but was always greater than that which I had received from the Stob. With each making a contribution to the household fund the occupants of the bungalow gave up a long austerity and began to eat and drink more like civilised people.

At frequent intervals Edward came to feast longing eyes upon his beloved but he still pressed his suit in an over-modest and self-obliterating fashion. Joan and I were sure that the thing would only end in marriage if Edward either became masterful or forced Arabella into compliance by the thought that she might lose him.

There was going to be a Ball in the hotel at Nethy Bridge, a neighbouring Spey Valley village, and it was to be given by a branch of the Freemasons. The women set their hearts on it and Edward was summoned to attend along with Randall and myself. I never learned to dance for I was too shy as a boy to clasp young women, and too clumsy as a man, but I knew that there would be drink and jolly company.

After a whole day spent in mannequin parades, displays of temperament, misgivings, satisfactions, discarded and reinstated dresses, we had a round of whisky of a choice brand provided by Edward and issued forth into the permafrost. It was an excruciatingly cold night with a light covering of snow on black ice. In those days, and in that place, salt was only used for porridge and potatoes and sand was reserved for the steepest road gradients. The roads through the valleys were as smooth and polished as the Cresta bob sleigh run.

When our two cars slid to a halt outside the hall the Ball was already under way. A local band was hammering away and much of the population of the Spey valley were dancing in the enormous room. The two couples paired off at once and were lost to sight in the gyrating mob. Feeling a little left out of things I went to find solace at the bar.

Soon I was mellow and philosophical, sharp and witty. I supposed I ought to circulate a bit although it was pretty certain I would find nobody I knew. In that I was wrong. I saw his face across a crowded room, a thin, clerkish face, meanly attired in a pair of National Health spectacles. Here was a bear to bait. I pushed myself towards him, displacing half-canned rustics on the way. When I stood before him there was no spark of recognition: 'Mr Chamber-Pot, fancy finding you here. You must remember me!'

'Eh?' Like all bears he was monosyllabic.

'Mr Chamber-Pot, the Man from the Ministry. The Department of Stealth and Sexual Depravity.'

He was vaguely stung. 'That's not my name. Who are you?'

We were soon exchanging insults. 'You said I was drunk', I accused, quite unbending, 'which, I submit, is a case of the Pot calling the Kettle black. I bet *you* can't even remember the number of your car.'

'Can you?' said Chambers, bridling a bit.

'I can't afford a car. I could, if it wasn't for your damn stamps. I came here on home-made skis', I added inventively.

'Oh, I see.' People only believe me when I say the silliest things. 'I am sorry about that. Hope things'll improve for you. But if you think I'm the worst for drink – well, my car number is MIN 320, a Ford Popular. Nice little job, bought her last year.'

'Good for you,' I made a supreme effort to commit the number to memory. It sank in the grey matter beneath a cushion of fumes. 'You're OK, that's clear enough. Now let's cry pax. I'd like to make up for my rudeness by buying you a drink. Come on, let's go to the bar. Even the Germans and the British once had a Christmas truce.'

I fed him a small dram, grudging every penny it cost me, excused myself and went in search of Randall. He was leaning between two pillars of imitation marble telling a spellbound young receptionist how he had encountered the Big Grey Man of Ben Macdhui, a figure of local legend. I waited until he had reached the punch line of his lying tale, then barged in on them. 'Peter', I said, and nodded to the terrified girl, 'please excuse this interruption. Are you fit for a ploy?'

'Any time, old man.'

'Come on then, we have to go outside. I'll tell you as we go.'

MIN 320 was not hard to find: it looked just like its owner, small, dark and fussily inefficient. Its headlamps were as close together as his eyes.

It was hard to believe that Chambers would be the kind of man to leave his car unlocked, but he had. Peter began to rub his hands together. 'Just look at that.' He pointed to a large shed which lay, with wide doors agape, right in the path of MIN 320. 'You steer, I'll push: your man from the Ministry probably forgot his anti-freeze. He'll thank us for putting her under cover – when he finds her!'

There was a perfect end to our plan. The shed, apart from its central passage, was stacked with bales of hay. We found a tarpaulin and carefully draped it over the car, then packed the bales around it until it was as snug as a bug in a rug. As a parting gesture we closed the big doors behind us.

As we went back into the hotel we met Arabella. 'Come quickly', she said, 'and see this; Joan's been enlisted.' This appeared to be true. There was a crowd of people clapping loudly round a small dais on which stood my wife, looking flushed and very pretty, with a large Masonic apron wrapped round her evening dress. It was a night of surprises.

An hour or two went by. In drinking situations people come and go as if by magic, the sudden return of lost friends is taken as much for granted as is their instant vanishing. It took the four of us, as a corporate body, a long time to realise that Edward had done the latter: comparing notes we concluded that nobody had seen him for ages. The women took this seriously. 'I don't think he was awfully well', said Joan. 'He was white-looking and wobbling when I saw him last'. Arabella said: 'He kissed me in front of the whole room. I didn't mind at all but it just wasn't Edward.'

'Pissed as a newt as observed by me', remarked Randall who tended to avoid involvement except when it suited him. 'He was working his way towards the loo by hanging on to the wall. That was more than an hour ago. No, don't get up ladies, this may not be a sight for pretty eyes. I shall go and look for him and call upon my friend Richard to help me if necessary.'

A few minutes later I saw him beckoning me from the door. I went over and he whispered in my ear: 'Try to keep a straight face, Richard', he said, 'I think Edward's dying.'

'Good God, why?'

'The drink's poisoned him. I never thought of him as a drinking man and I just don't think he had the constitution for it.'

'Had? Don't say that!'

Inside the Gents there was the usual arrangement of porcelain compartments with a gutter for the urine. Edward lay in the middle of the gutter. It was a measure of the kind of man he was that even in these adverse circumstances he still wore an air of quiet dignity and self-abasement. And like Mark Twain's his state had been grossly exaggerated for as we watched he began to rise to his feet by bracing his back against the smooth porcelain. Alas, just as he was about to stand erect the flushing jets gurgled spitefully and he went down again under a miniature Niagara. Randall and I were so shocked by the sight that for a few moments we could do nothing to help. Then we dragged him from the waterfall and propped his soaking body against a wall. The bite of the cold water had brought him round. Randall loosened his tie and wiped his face dry with a filthy towel he had found lying on the floor. Much sooner than we expected he regained the power of speech, his first thought, as ever, being for others: 'I can't start to apologise for this disgusting performance. I'm sure I shouldn't drive and I'd hate Arabella or Joan to see me like this. They'd be terribly offended. Peter – I simply hate to ask this – but would you drive me home?'

'Of course, old man. Absolutely no sweat.' I went to inform the women of our intention and reassure them. Edward was a trifle under the weather. We would see him safely home and then come back.

I rejoined the pair of them. Edward, normally a modest smoker, had taken a cigarette and was pushing it against his face in an effort to find his mouth. Randall guided him and casually flicked his lighter. All might have been well had the cigarette been untipped but as it was Randall lit the cork and Edward's first inhalation brought on a terrible spasm of coughing. It was too much for him: he swayed, buckled at the knees and collapsed in the other's arms.

'That's the end of him', said Randall, 'for a while. He's out for the count now.' He lowered Edward to the ground. 'Give us a hand to get him to the car.'

Neither of us was fit to carry him but he dragged quite easily along the frozen ground. 'He'll have to go in the middle', said Randall. 'The door catch is worn and if it opens we'll lose him.' It was a tight fit in the narrow car but at length we arranged ourselves and set off along the icy road. Almost at once Edward began to moan in his sleep.

'Why's he doing that?' asked Randall irritably. 'We've done our best for him. Make him shut up. That's a filthy noise.'

'I think the poor brute's cold. And probably feeling sick.'

'Not in here, I hope.' He looked down. 'No it's not that. He's being gelded by the gear lever.'

As lusty men we saw the importance of this, and stopped. What to do now? I had an instant brainwave. 'Put him in the boot. It's quite big enough and he won't need much air for the ten minutes it'll take to get home.'

'Good scheme. Let's do that. Anyway I'm bursting for a pee.'

Out there, in the flat bottom of the glen, it was bitterly cold. Evening clothes are unsuited to zero temperatures and only the ample amount of alcohol in our blood, acting like anti-freeze, protected us against its full impact. Yet, at the same time, it addled our senses like a blow to the head: I had not realised how very drunk I was. Thus deranged we did things out of sequence and had laid Edward in the road behind the boot, preparatory to loading him, before we went to empty our bladders, coyly standing back to back on opposite sides of the road.

It had become pink elephant time for both of us, intentions and facts were merged together in our fiery brains. Why else did the moon dance an uneasy jig in the sky, and why else did I ever afterwards remember in the clearest detail fitting the helpless Edward into the MG's boot amid a tangle of fencing wire, bags of staples and the other tools of our trade?

As we slid to a halt outside the Bungalow we heard the telephone ringing in the house. 'Get him out', I said, 'I'll answer the damn thing.' It was my wife, sounding disenchanted. 'Don't bother to come back. Arabella and I will come in Edward's car. It's all rather a bore, there're just a bunch of drunken fools messing about and a stupid little man who says his car's been stolen.'

'Oh good!'

'What's that?'

'I said, oh my God. It must be trying for you.'

'It is. Get the kettle on for a cup of tea, will you?'

'Will do. Wait a minute, don't ring off. There's Peter shouting about something. Maybe he's forgotten his coat.'

It was not, of course, his coat that had been forgotten and when, seconds later, I briskly concluded my talk with Joan she must have noticed the change in my voice. Her last words were: 'What do you mean, we're not to come home? How can the road be blocked by an avalanche – it's not that kind of road. No, Peter and you are up to something. Just see that there's a good cup of tea for us or there'll be trouble!'

Edward hadn't moved. He lay right in the middle of the road. A small wind was whispering round him and had blown loose snow upon his face and hair. We approached him with the deference due to the dead. Peter tried to feel his heart but wasn't able to get his hand through the frost-stiff coat. 'I'm afraid he's gone. You've . . .'

'What do you mean, "I've"? You didn't put him in either. That's not the way to find out anyway. Put your hand on his mouth, then you'll see if he's breathing. Now, is he sucking?'

'He's sucking. Thank God for that!'

'Thank God for it, indeed.' Relief made me quite hysterical. 'Can you imagine Arabella's face if she'd run him over? What an end to the great romance!'

Faithful Bob, disturbed by our lightning visit, was up and had made the tea. He had also stoked the Rayburn to white heat. We tried to undress Edward in front of it but only a hammer would have softened his frozen clothes. He was now semi-conscious and muttering and seemed to appreciate our ministrations. He had been lying across two benches and we were sliding him to and fro against the warm glow of the fire. We had finished his front and were just starting on the other side when Joan and Arabella came in. They were both anxious and angry.

'What madness is that?' demanded Joan, 'you've dropped him in the snow, you drunken louts. Come on, Bob, have we got a hot bottle for Mr Edward? He'll get his death of cold. I think we ought to ring up Dr Macdonald.'

This was practical Joan, at her best, but Arabella surpassed herself. She knelt beside Edward's bier and took his bloodless hand in hers. She touched his cracked lips with her own. 'Oh my poor Edward', she murmured, 'what a bitch I've been to you. I'll make it up to you, I promise.' Tears pricked my eyes at this touching scene but Randall, insensitive beast that he was, doubled up with laughter: 'Father Christmas has found a mate at last.'

It would be nice to record here that they were married the next day by special licence. It took a little longer than that. But they were married in the end and Edward took her to live in the far north of Canada where he works out the tax problems of the Esquimaux. Some men are gluttons for nostalgia. As for Mr Chambers, it was rumoured that he suffered a nervous breakdown and retired early from being a public nuisance. At any rate I never saw him again.

9 ✤ *The Ill Wind*

We finished our first fence. It was half a mile long and straight as a die, and we were proud of it. A good fence is a pleasing feature of the countryside, and this was one of the best. It began on a sheep-cropped patch of grass, mounted a rocky knoll, dipped its wooden legs in a peaty hollow, passed through a birch wood and ended, as it began, in a stout pillar of peeled golden pine. It was satisfying work and I was beginning to enjoy it.

'No more fencing for the moment, old man', announced Peter Randall, the next day.

'Don't say that! What are we going to do now?'

'No cause for alarm. Mr Jackson wants me to do some thinning.'

'What about me?'

'Well, you too, naturally. Don't think for a moment – You know that this is a joint effort. But he spoke about this when I first called on him and before I had a chance to mention you. He gave me some tips. It sounds quite amusing. I shall be selecting trees for the final crop and deciding on those which have to come out.'

'That's still you. Where do I come in?'

'Well, just for the moment – just until you pick up the idea – will you carry the paint pot and brush? We're not allowed to use an axe. Daub the trees which I point out.'

'Not very demanding. How about the money?'

'Split down the middle, as always.'

Randall was so good at thinning trees that I suspected him of taking secret lessons from the woods' manager. There was a deeply devious side to his nature which continually found expression in quite unnecessary concealments. It was impossible to judge at times what made him do this or what personal advantage he hoped to gain.

The work was, as he said, quite amusing. The aim was

to ensure a perfect crop of pine and it was impossible not to compare our method of selection to that of an autocratic dictator blackly dedicated to the improvement of a conquered country. For instance, we sentenced the 'whips' to death, and the 'whips' were the counterpart of thin young men about town, of no benefit to the race or the forest, who swung about drunkenly in high winds and knocked the limbs off their more worthy neighbours. Then there were the runts, a few miserable feet in height, who lived out their short lives amid the undergrowth and were an affront to decent timber. In contrast were the wolves who had succeeded only too well. Gnarled, knotted and random branched, these were the profiteers of the wood, but though they might seem to flourish now they would bring little profit at the day's end for the timber was too short and twisted to be good for anything but boat-ends and boomerangs. Finally came those who had suffered great misfortune at the teeth of the grey squirrel. With their leaders severed in youth they had expended their energy in a bursting spray of side branches leaving only a dead, grey spike, like a unicorn's horn, above a bulbous excrescence.

Those that remained were dominant, full-bodied, clean limbed and straight of trunk: the members of the chosen race who were to live on in dignity to become the final crop.

It was an unusually mild January and we were grateful for it. The seven-mile journey to the wood which was situated on high ground above the upper Dulnain Valley would have been onerous in wintry conditions, even impossible in deep snow and our contract of work was payment by the acre. There was no bad weather money. As it was the bland days started with magic mornings. When we came to the wood it was still dark and we lit a great fire in the place where we kept our kettle. A thousand rabbits lived beside that wood – the 'white blindness' as Richard Adams calls it in *Watership Down* was still many years ahead – and we could see the flash of their eyes in the light of our torches and hear the scattering patter of their feet. Often the wood was misty. As we warmed ourselves by the fire and drank

our mugs of tea we could hear pigeons talking and sometimes a capercaillie would smash his blind, clumsy way
through the branches above us. The smell of wet pine
needles and the bog myrtle we had bruised beneath our
boots was nectar sweet: not so, and only fit for nostalgia,
was the stench of a group of Phallus impudicus which stood
near by. Though now well crumbled they still held the
strange form of rampant male desire as they exhibited
themselves coarsely to a few shocked early primroses.

Within a fortnight we had covered most of the wood. Mr
Jackson came to inspect our work and was well pleased.
Sitting by the fire and taking tea with us he assured us of
almost unlimited work ahead, for the timber markets were
steadily picking up and he had a huge thinning programme
in front of him. I felt like taking a deep, grateful breath and
thanking whatever patron saint is allocated to those who
grope their ways through life. Things were looking up. The
Bungalow was out of debt, Joan and I had jolly company
and the chance of amusing occasions, there was unlimited
opportunity to visit the mountains with my companion
who, at least in that context, never put a foot wrong. Lastly,
and not without importance, I had shown my mother that I
could stand alone.

January crept to its end on the pussy feet of warm air.
The sense of Spring was all pervasive. On the evening of the
30th, I remarked to Randall, 'Let's go to the cinema
tonight, and take the girls. It's time we relaxed.' We took an
early train and descended en masse upon my mother. The
Old Woman was in rare form. Joan and she had entered a
period of détente, she liked Arabella whom she saw through
warped romantic eyes as an agreeable threat to her son's
marriage, and she had warmed to Randall whom she had
once regarded as an unwelcome addition to her support
plan. He was at his best with older women. He jumped up
and down every time she came into the room and offered his
lighter, though never his cigarettes, with monotonous regu-
larity: in exchange for her whisky he agreed with every
word she said.

After the cinema we caught the midnight train home. It was the weirdest night imaginable, so warm on the high ground that it might have been taken for summer. We stood around in the Bungalow garden wondering at it and looking up at the sky where a whirling fretwork of tornado-shaped clouds stood waving their tails towards the west. Up there was tumult but not a breath of wind stirred the bare branches of the birches. 'I wonder what it means?' asked Randall, 'it looks like the onset of some cosmic disaster.' He could never resist a bit of drama.

We took tea with Bob, kissed a sleeping Richard good-night and went to our beds.

I am sure that everybody has had the experience of waking up to such abnormal darkness that he thinks he has gone blind. I had it, that morning. In the Bungalow it was never perfectly dark for the lights from the railway cast a suffused glow: not, at least, until then. With a huge shock of panic I groped for the electric light switch and clicked it on. Nothing. Darkness, like black satin before my eyes. I struggled out of bed and tried to push open the window. It wouldn't budge. Joan had woken up with all my commotion. 'What's wrong – oh, how dark it is. Where are you? Why don't you put on the light?' She tried, then added: 'I've a match – wait.' There was a scrape and a small glorious flame set the shadow dancing in the room.

The window, an outward-opening casement, was held fast by a wall of snow. We could hear the steady roar of an oddly muted wind. 'Good God!' I said, 'we're buried. There's a blizzard blowing. I'll find a torch and see what's going on.'

Now I knew that I wasn't blind the whole thing was a big adventure. I went through the house and opened the back door. It opened easily enough, for the wind was coming from the west and it faced north. The snow was shallow here but over the Bungalow roof it was a rushing plume of unbroken white, countless millions of swollen flakes joined edge to edge in a single corporate movement. I flashed the torch in the direction of the forest and as its light vaguely encircled a crown the tree fell away and vanished. I wondered about our wood on the high ground above the valley.

I went back to Joan: 'Richard? Is he all right?'

'Sleeping like a little pig. They all are.'

'I suppose there's no chance of tea?'

'I love your sense of humour. You know what heats an electric kettle.'

'Fool. I meant the Rayburn.'

'Gone out. I think the chimney's blocked by snow.'

'Oh God. What time is it?'

'Ask Him direct. He may answer. The telephone won't say a thing.'

'You have a watch, haven't you? Oh dear, do we have to go on living here?'

'My watch is in Peter's car. So let's forget it's happening and go back to sleep.'

'You enjoy this sort of thing' she accused, 'as far as I'm concerned, it's no joke.'

She was, as usual, right. It was no joke. Just how unfunny it was we didn't learn until we dug our way into Randall's MG (buried under four feet of snow) and switched on his old crackler of a radio. Then we heard that the Larne ferry boat had foundered in a tumult of green water with the loss of many lives; falling trees and flying chimney pots had caused death and injury and thousands of trees had been uprooted.

On the west side the Bungalow was flush with the snow. It was fifteen feet deep. Randall and I put on our rucksacks and waded thigh high to the village to get essential stores. There was much devastation. Telephone wires were down and some poles had been snapped off. The twisted wires concealed beneath the snow made walking difficult. Many of the big Scots pine had been decapitated with such force that their crowns had been carried several hundred feet away from the boles.

We went back to the Bungalow where Bob had lit two huge fires. We lit candles in every room to keep our spirits up. Outside the short day faded and a hard frost came to petrify a tableau of destruction.

As soon as the telephone was restored we phoned Mr Jackson. The woods' manager was distracted. It seemed, in the circumstances, very bad taste to mention the word 'thinnings', like discussing arsenic with a man who has been accidently poisoned and is still sick from it, but the call had to start somewhere. Mr Jackson was less than forthcoming. When Randall finally pushed the point the woods' manager was heard to mutter: 'Thinnings? You just don't understand, do you? Get along that road and have a look at my wood. That'll teach you to be fatuous!'

Two days later we went there, driving through a narrow snow corridor with walls ten feet high. It was hard to know where to stop. The whole country had changed. Twice we concluded that we must have misjudged the place but when at last we knew where we were we could still hardly believe our eyes. The twenty-acre forest had contained about fifteen hundred trees; we could vouch for that figure, we had computed it ourselves from sample plots. Because the wood had stood on the exposed crown of a hill we had expected the damage to be extensive. But not this! It was as though a giant matchbox had been emptied onto the ground. Trees lay in chaotic positions, some flat on the all-embracing snow, others propped high across their neighbours' backs. In areas of general collapse some crowns had been pinned down under such weight that the trunks were lifted high in the air and their roots brandished like tattered black flags. In a shocked, disbelieving silence we made our count of those which remained upstanding. It was thirty seven trees.

Perversely, but not without reason, each one carried our mark. Many of them were wolves. The massive root systems had held them erect though some of them had lost most of their limbs. They resembled rough-hewn telephone poles. The whips, too, had come off well: they were too slim to have offered over-much resistance to the snow-laden wind. Despite the totality of the destruction we guessed that the death of the forest had taken place within a few minutes. From the general lie of the timber it was clear that the heavily branched outside trees to windward had collapsed under the weight of snow and brought down with them the whole forest in one single, deadly ripple.

'Like nine-pins', I suggested to Randall. 'I wouldn't like to have the counting of this lot.'

'Nor would I', said he, 'but I reckon that's what's expected of us. Mr Jackson hinted as much through his tears. I've a feeling that he wants us to start tomorrow.'

So we counted, and counted, and filled notebooks with our figures. We moved from wood to wood. At the end of February we added our count to the swelling national total. In the north-east alone it then stood at more than a million cubic feet. We went into the grounds of Castle Grant, a residence of the Lords of Seafield, where some of the finest living members of the species Pinus sylvestris had been brought down. These huge trees were special and had to be measured so that their yield might be computed.

The timber trade was in confusion. The felling of mature timber was tightly controlled by the Board of Trade and established bureaucratic rulings are hard to bend. It remained an offence to fell one's own tree in one's own garden and though this prohibition sprang from a sensible policy – the restoration of timber after the massive fellings of the recent war it was now without point. But the planners were adamant: until the count was complete the dead forests must lie as they fell, untouched. As time went on the timber merchants and the woodsmen grew uneasy: they, the men on the spot, knew full well that if the cutters did not soon get busy the beetle and the fungus, oblivious to officialdom, would do so.

In the end the total count for the whole country was six million cubic feet, a million trees, more or less. On the triplicate forms of the Felling Licences the 'number of trees scheduled' was left blank and the signature at the bottom was God's.

10 ❧ *Variations on a Familiar Theme*

Sardines, living in a tin, are only happy because they are dead and the six of us (Bob and Richard making up the score) had been too long together in too small a space. Tensions were building up in the Bungalow. Sultry atmospheres were only cleared by the lightning of sharp words and the occasional thunderous outburst, while reconciliations were the falsest of dawns. A final storm was brewing up.

It began on a note of minor complaint. Peter Randall who still monopolised negotiations with Mr Jackson suddenly informed me that our business with the woods' manager was ended. He added, without a blush, that he had fixed himself up with a job on the West Coast as manager of a small sawmill. Such treachery made the bile rise in my throat and I remarked with much restraint: 'How unexpected! When will you go?' 'In a fortnight', he said, and added the usual rider: 'If I might stay until . . .'

'Certainly not!' said Joan with whose spokesmanship I heartily concurred, 'You've made use of us long enough. You can go at once.' He had the grace not to argue but it came as a surprise to me when Arabella said to Joan: 'Come on, you can't throw him out like that.'

'Oh yes, I can. And while we're having a Spring clean I think we'd like the house to ourselves. I won't rush you, but please make other arrangements.' When it comes to emotions, I thought, women are rather like pressure cookers: they boil silently before blowing off steam. While the women exchanged recriminations Randall and I, typical male cowards, slunk away and drank whisky in his room. He didn't expand on his defection or the reasons for it but handed me my share of the money we had put aside for the mountaineering magazine. The next day they both left without forwarding addresses.

We heard from Arabella years later when she and Edward were married and living with the Esquimaux but that strange man Randall has been silent for nigh on thirty years.

But I go too fast. By next morning Joan and I, by the help of some applied bio-chemistry and much reassuring talk, were on excellent terms again and I was ready to agree that it was nice to be on our own, a condition which always included Bob. He, dear man, seeing a complacency on my part which could easily lead to a slide back into debt immediately proposed a plan of his own. It was that he and I should look for a contract cutting timber. With the windblows still thick on the ground such work was easy to get. But, he hastened to add, the arrangement must be in my name; he who of all men was most entitled to my confidence never presumed on recognition. He would work for me and find two others to do the same.

We were offered a contract at once. It was to cut up some huge Scots Pine windblows which had fallen on a hill-top near Dulnain Bridge, a village some ten miles away. He was equally quick in finding two men. Both lived in Carr Bridge but neither was indigenous. The elder, a dark faced, saturnine man, hailed from Glasgow. His name was Archie McTurk. He was a steady worker but he had a stubborn regard for the exact letter of his employment and was a major loss to the trades unions. The other man, in his early thirties, was a Newfie, as they were locally called, who had come with the timber squads during the war and had married a local wench. He was called Kelogg: he had no Christian name, being recorded in the Electorial Roll as – Kelogg. In the absence of any other of that name in the north of Scotland this was adequate. He was a husky, happy man with an animal's pleasure in using his body, a fact to which his incessantly pregnant wife would no doubt testify. His German parents had settled in Newfoundland after the First War and from them he had inherited a strong Teutonic accent. He had few words and the two phrases he used in general communication – 'Iss verr goot' or 'Iss na goot at a' – were sufficient to get him by in the undemanding society in which he lived. What he lacked in learning he made up for in geniality and he had a drive to work which would have shamed a bulldozer.

Today a skilled man using a powerful chainsaw can cut down a whole forest in next to no time but in 1953 these things were in their infancy. For the most part they were heavy, cumbersome and unreliable and the two-man crosscut saw still reigned supreme. Accordingly the men came in pairs with their beautifully kept and sharpened tool and a couple of snedding axes. They were paid for their work by the cubic foot, a measure of the heartwood in the log when the limbs were removed and the piece cut to a prescribed length. The contractor's arithmetic was basically simple: he paid the cutters as little as they would take and demanded from the timber merchant as much as he would give. His profit lay in the difference less the cost of transporting the men to work (or housing them in rough sheds on the site), paying them time rates between contracts or when the weather made work impossible, and the cost of his own time as an unpaid agent of the Inland Revenue in working out PAYE and National Insurance contributions. But since this margin was only a penny or two the contractor, unless he was in a big way of business, had to take a partner and work himself.

Bob, naturally, was my partner; and also my instructor. Like most beginners in this exercise I used brute strength to pull and bear down upon the saw and it was some days before I learnt that a light touch and a smooth raking action achieved the best results.

To take ourselves and our two men to the job we had had to find some form of transport. A van would have been ideal, but after years of hazardous adventuring on Bizarro Joan and I thought we owed ourselves a treat. After all it was to be our first car. The choice, however, of a 1936 Fraser Nash BMW was more exciting than practical. It was also, knowing me, dismally predictable, comparable to my headlong purchase of the Bungalow. I have always been besotted by the unusual. The car, the subject of a hire purchase agreement, was a sturdy two-door saloon painted battleship-grey with a six-cylinder Meadows engine which could take it up to 90 m.p.h. Its rock-hard suspension and solid chassis enabled it to hold this speed even on the tightest corners. It had, indeed, only one serious drawback: bolder men than I had bombed the BMW factory during the war and its spares availability was nil. At the time I took delivery it was going perfectly so the significance of this made no impression on me at all.

We picked up the men on a sparkling March morning. 'Iss verr goot car, this thing', boomed Kelogg when I smilingly told him it was of German origin like himself. 'Musta cost yer', said McTurk rudely, and I could imagine his avaricious mind regretting the rate per cubic foot which we had agreed. In no time at all we reached the edge of the wood, parked the car in a lane and carried our tools up to the trees. They looked monstrous under a grey covering of rime. As we took up position on either side of the trunks the great flame of the sun came up over the mountains to the east. It was all sparkling light and blue shadows.

When we started to saw we were dressed against the cold. Very soon jackets and sweaters were abandoned. Within an hour my shirt was hanging on a branch and through the dry air I could feel the hot touch of the sun on my back. It was intense physical pleasure, something worth living for. When the first four trees were severed from their roots we lit a roasting fire of dead fir limbs and rosy resin chips and made tea. It was smoky and scalding, the best tea in the whole world.

But there was a serpent in Eden. McTurk had begun to whine in his nasal Glasgow accent. 'We canna cut furthy doon the tree unless Macdonald', who was the timber merchant, 'sends up a tractor to move them blocks.' A twelve-foot log, as big as an elephant, had rolled down against another tree which was about to be cut. 'Wait you', whispered Bob, 'he'll ask you to put him on time. I'll tell him to start on another.' He did so but McTurk was by no means mollified. 'Wot aboot pying for yon cut then? It'll na be measured where it is. It'll na be pyed for this week. How aboot ma wife and ma bairns?'

Kelogg, however, was made of sterner stuff. 'It iss not goot we wait. Perhaps Macdonald no come. I move tree, no nonsense more.' It was a big speech for him but it had not drained his strength. He kicked his heels into the hard ground and put his broad back against the log. The veins in his honest forehead stood out like earth worms on a tennis court and the log rolled a few feet up hill. Kelogg breathed deeply: 'You haf not a gut, Turk', he grinned. 'Now is no nonsense more!' McTurk was deeply shocked: 'You're not pyed to move them trees', he said, 'just to cut 'em.'

We were soon looking for another contract. The first one had turned out well. Even McTurk was pleased with his share of the cube and both men wanted to go on working for us. At once I answered an advertisement in a local paper. By return of post I had a reply which asked me to meet a Mr Ian Macdonald at a wood near Moy (a village ten miles distant) that very afternoon. Mr Macdonald was obviously not one for wasting time.

He was a plain-spoken person with devil's eyebrows and a passion for motor rallying. When I had introduced myself and Bob he remarked: 'You'll be Mr Frere's son then?' with what I took to be a slight sneer. It seemed to imply a fall from grace on my part but he went on in a friendly enough fashion, 'That's a fine car you've got there' and would not get down to business until I had given him all its particulars. Then he said abruptly, 'We'll look over the wood. I want it felled, cross-cut and pulled out to the loading banks. You'll need a horse if you haven't one already. My price is seven and a half pence the cubic foot.'

'On the bank?' I said, playing for time. Naturally he would be ready to bargain.

'That's right. You don't think I'd pay for it lying up there. You'd probably go off and leave me with it. Then I'd have to pay another man to get it down.'

'I wouldn't do that.'

'Probably not. But one doesn't take chances.'

'Well, on the bank I couldn't do it for less than nine pence a foot.'

'That's bad luck then.'

'How do you mean.'

'I mean, my price is sevenpence-halfpenny. That's bad luck for you.'

'Well, let's say eight pence', I faltered.

'You can say it. But my price is sevenpence-halfpenny. Good-day to you, Mr Frere. I've enjoyed our chat but I'm a busy man. Don't think I'm rude but I fancy you've not had much experience in the timber trade. If you had you'd know there's damn-all margin of profit and with all these trees lying around it'll be tighter still. Now that's a fine car you've got: drive around the country and enjoy it. Don't tell me you can't afford to. Your father was no pauper and well-known in the town. Chaps like you lose their money larking around where they don't belong. I had this business handed me on a plate but *my* father started from scratch . . .'

'Sevenpence-halfpenny will do', I said. 'Between ourselves the car isn't half paid for.'

He gave me a surprised look. 'Oh, well. I suppose things change. If you must, you must. You'll find me a fair man to work for. Most of my contractors do well. But have a word of advice – watch the men you take on. They're a sharp lot and'll bleed you white given half a chance. You're in the jungle in more ways than one', he ended with a bleak smile.

After that I let Bob do the talking. Ian Macdonald, or John Oak as he was affectionately known, saw that Bob knew what he was about and they settled the details between them.

We had to get a horse who was used to pulling timber. I knew nothing about such horses; where you found them, how much they cost, what they ate or what equipment they needed. Bob did, and I left it all to him.

Dobbin (he had been christened Prince but we suspected sarcasm and dropped the name) came to us for three pounds a week and an option to purchase. We met him on a

fine April morning when he kicked open the door of the
cattle float which had brought him to the wood. He
appeared to be in a foul temper. After giving us a show of
yellow teeth he made for the nearest patch of grass and
cropped it savagely. 'Got spirit', announced Bob in a satisfied voice. I shrugged my shoulders for I could feel no
confidence in the surly beast.

McTurk and Kelogg had been working for three days.
There were many piles of cut logs ready for pulling. It
struck me that I must already owe the cutters a lot of money
and I had doubts that Dobbin would make it possible for
me to get mine. Apart from the illness of his nature he was
not a big horse and he seemed quite dwarfed by the scale of
the operation.

The wood lay along the top of a steep bank which formed
one side of a small glen. An estate road, up which Oak's
lorries would come, ran up its middle. Once on top of the
bank the timber would roll down to the road. All the horse
had to do was to pull the timber to the edge. But the logs
were big and numerous and I could not see it happening.

Dobbin seemed to share my misgivings. He had pointedly turned his back to the wood and was wolfing great
quantities of grass like a deprived rabbit. While he did so
Bob laid out the dragging equipment on the road and
explained to me how it worked. It all looked so heavy and
awkward that I was sure the horse would get entangled in
its chains and break his legs at once. Then he would have to
be shot.

'We'll get the collar on', said Bob, 'when he's ready.' He
allowed Dobbin another ten minutes feeding then took the
collar to his head. As he saw its approach the horse pushed
his nose between his front legs. Bob gave him a sharp slap
on the rump, the horse looked up with a kind of outrage and
the collar was up and over. He stamped his hooves irritably
as Bob hooked the chains to it.

'Right, horse, let's have you then', remarked Bob
equably. Dobbin shuddered. 'Go on, gee up!' The creature
tottered as though exhausted even by the idea. Without

further exhortation Bob took out his knife and sliced a thin wand from a birch coppice. He laid it on the ground where Dobbin could see it. The beast showed a royal disdain. Bob picked up the stick and swished the air with it. At that Dobbin got the message and took to his heels, clanking his chains on the stony ground like Marley's ghost affrighted. 'You see that', grinned Bob, greatly delighted: 'he's no fool but he wants us to think it was *his* idea. They don't like losing face.'

A few minutes later we were on top of the hill and ready for the real test. On seeing the first pile of logs Dobbin began to tremble violently. 'Now what's wrong with him?' I asked suspiciously. 'Just keen to start, that's all', reassured Bob. 'Oh I see.' I had, in fact, made quite a different interpretation.

'Now we'll find him a good stick.' Bob selected a twelve-foot length which had been cut right from the bottom of a forest giant. It must have weighed a quarter of a ton. I transferred some of my sympathy to the horse. 'He'll never move that! You'll kill him', I said. 'Nonsense', scoffed Bob, 'Holy Old Smoke, he is a *horse*, isn't he?' and at the words the garron nodded his head several times. More than once in our acquaintance I was to have reason to suspect a touch of circus ancestry.

It took both of us much sweat and the use of a stout lever to raise the end of the log high enough to encircle it with the chain. Bob said smartly – 'Gee up, go', and the horse edged forward until he felt the weight. At once a dramatic change came over him. He grew in stature, his formerly smooth flanks sported ridges of muscles, he dug in his rear hooves and clawed the ground with his front. The log moved forward and gathered momentum like a high-speed electric train leaving its platform. Though its passage was impeded by small roots and boulders Dobbin did not slack his pace until Bob stopped him on the very edge of the hill. I was abject in my shame at how I had undervalued this unshorn Samson.

By that evening all the cut logs were lying on the floor of

the glen and Dobbin was waiting scornfully for McTurk and Kelogg. It was obvious that as the forest shrank back from the edge of the hill the drags would become longer but Dobbin had moved the product of three days' cutting in a single afternoon and unless we brought in more men to fell more trees the horse would soon enjoy the trades union dream of a two day week. We took on four more good men, and were lucky to find them. By the third week we had sent a dozen heavily loaded lorries to Inverness and I picked up my first pay packet. It was as thick as a *Who's Who*. After I had recovered money from wages already paid, deducted tax, bought National Stamps (with the ghost of Chambers always at my shoulder) and paid for Dobbin's feed there remained a lot of cash.

It now seemed sensible to get a lad to help Bob with Dobbin and in due course to take full charge of the horse. Bob and I had roving commissions and what with marking, measuring and setting up the timber on its loading bank as well as handling Dobbin, we were fully occupied. We let it be known that we wanted a school leaver with an interest in horses who was prepared to do what he was told. Twenty-four hours later we had one.

Charlie McBurn was seventeen years old, tall for his age, shock haired and encrusted with acne. He was a lonely lad, the kind who are naturally 'got at' by their mates and for that reason had failed to hold down any of the seventeen jobs he had tried since leaving school. He was pathetically anxious to get this job and keep it: he later confided to Bob that his crofter father was a harsh tyrant who beat him black and blue each time he came home with his cards. Bob saw that in the matter of Charlie we were in a buyer's market and engaged him at a pittance, less than half our weekly outlay on Dobbin. The horse took an instant dislike to the boy. A proud beast, he would take orders from calm, mature and confident Bob but he held a contemptuous view of Charlie who blustered and cajoled. Each time the lad came into range – being rather dim, he did so quite often – he gave him a ritual kick. Charlie never seemed to learn.

Lifted by the garron's powerful hooves, he was flung in all directions and I pondered on how violent a man his father must be that the boy would continue to accept the horse's savagery without a thought of packing in the job.

The April days began to lengthen. In the little glen the birches turned rosy and then green, and on the bank saws hissed and axes rang from twilight to twilight. At the steady onslaught of the six woodsmen the wall of standing timber fell back as corn before the sickle. John Oak's big lorries came as empty virgins and left as pregnant matrons, their steel-strapped wombs bulging with timber, and the money rolled in. It was all too good to be true.

It had been an unusually dry April with a constant cold east wind and in early May a hot sun began to shine. The litter of limbs from hundreds of felled trees began to bother Dobbin and I suggested to Bob that we might burn away some of the tangle in order to give the horse a clear run to the top of the bank. Bob was adamant that we should not do so. 'You'd never stop it in this weather, the ground's as dry as a cork', he cautioned. I agreed in words but could not dismiss the idea from my mind. Each person, I submit, has the embryo of some obsession in his subconscious which is held in check by social, legal or religious considerations. In my case it is pyromania. I love to see things crackle and flare up. I am a latent arsonist. But it could not be done in cold blood, I had to give Fate an opening, the chance to take a hand in my dark design. So the next morning, carelessly but without intent, I lit my cigarette and dropped an unextinguished match into the centre of a pile of brash. There were no logs within twenty yards and if it caught it would purge a useful area of ground.

It caught. In the hot sun it was not even possible to see the first wild spread of the fire as it leaped into a widening bubble of heat. As I still stared stupidly at the point of origin the flames were all around me. Within seconds the whole area I had selected was a roaring inferno. I jumped out of the way and shouted an alarm.

Bob gave me an accusing look and took control at once.

Already a few men had rushed through the smoke and were beating the flames with branches. Such unconcerted action did more harm than good for as each branch came down it set up a cloud of sparks which ignited their own fires. Bob directed the men to isolate the area by dragging branches out of the way and making fire breaks. It slowed the fire but did not stop it; the ground was thick with matted twigs and dead grass and the burning perimeter had expanded like a ripple in a pond. We were a very Thin Red Line.

Somewhere in the smoke Dobbin and Charlie had been having their tea break. The horse had withdrawn smartly but of the boy there was no sign at all. He was known to take a nap at such times and in my guilt ridden panic I saw that I had promoted a holocaust for him. It was with untold relief that I saw him spring up behind a fire burst and run for his life.

The men were doing what they could but they were outmatched. The fire was completely out of control. Logs which had been awaiting Dobbin's attention stood charred, the drier ones smoking darkly as the stored resin in their hearts oozed through the blackened bark. Bob, as black as any log, came over to me. He was sticky with sweat and streaked with charcoal and one of his trouser legs was smouldering. 'They're losing heart', he shouted, 'they say you'll lose the contract and they might as well go home now. But give 'em encouragement to stay and we might stop it yet.'

'How can we do that?' I mumbled.

'Get beer', he shouted, 'from the pub at Moy. And let me tell them it'll be double time for fire fighting.'

'Right, of course. I'll go at once.'

As I tumbled down the bank and jumped into the Fraser Nash I noticed that the sky which had been unbrokenly blue for days was suffused by a spreading grey stain. 'Thank God for that!' I murmured, 'let it rain soon.' I let in the clutch and went down the rough track as though all the devils in hell were on my tail.

I was back within half an hour. The car was heavy with

beer crates. At Moy the publican had at first demurred when I asked for immediate credit on half his stock but when I showed him the great black cloud that hung above the moor he had allowed it. Bob was waiting for me. He had Dobbin chained to a slipe, which is a rough sledge used for dragging timber. On this we loaded the beer and it was dragged up the hill to the wood.

Our men, inspired by the thought of immediate refreshment and a fat pay packet, now held the fire at bay. They had isolated the standing timber but though they had achieved victory on this front they had met defeat on another. The flames, fanned by a rising west wind, had reached the open moorland and were gobbling up acres of heather. At least a square mile was burned black and smooth. I was pretty sure that this was not the prescribed time to burn heather and sensed that I should now have to answer for my crimes to the estate owner as well as to John Oak.

Bob presided over the bar, flipping the caps off beer bottles and passing them to the parched men. The pace of the operation began to increase as afternoon turned to evening and the scene resembled a clip from a speeded-up movie. Men, zebra-striped and naked from the waist up, came in at a run, grabbed an opened bottle, emptied it and rushed back to duty. The line of fire had now been broken in a dozen places and final assaults were being made on isolated centres of resistance. Suddenly a new ally came to our aid. In the dense smoke the rain's approach had been unnoticed but now the heavens opened and a steady downpour began. The extensive damage would insure that I lose this contract and any other from John Oak but I felt a sense of exhilaration as I listened to the shouts of the firemen and the hiss of the dying flames. There was satisfaction in the knowledge of the good fight won. Over the moorland steam was replacing smoke but the men seemed indignant at the last-minute intervention of the rain when they, the few, had disputed the field so gallantly. So they went on thrashing doggedly at the embers.

Only two cases of beer remained unbreached. Bob gave me a glance and I nodded vigorously. The cry went up 'One for the road!' and it was closely followed by a burst of applause as Charlie was seen to discharge a pair of bottles into Dobbin's pail. The horse drank deeply and with obvious pleasure.

It was all over, the last flicker was dead. Some men, overcome by exhaustion, sat on the ground, their backs propped against blackened logs. Others lay supine in puddles of wet peat, empty bottles still clasped in their hands. It was a scene of high heroism that any Great Master would have been proud to paint. It was also the scene that met John Oak's eyes as he climbed to the top of the bank and gazed in blank disbelief at the acres of blackened ground and the stacks of smouldering logs. He had seen the pall of smoke from his house on the outskirts of Inverness.

He walked over to me, shrewdly assessing the loss. There was an angry frown on his face, but when he spoke it was with an odd note of satisfaction. 'I was right about you, Frere', he said, 'I thought you were this kind of man.' I didn't answer but tried to combine contrition and curiosity in the same expression. He answered my look: 'The kind who attracts trouble.' He mused. 'This is going to cost me a lot of money. The timber's insured but what about the moor?' His gaze shifted to my men, a few of whom tried to rise in the presence of the supreme power. Then I saw that John Oak's mouth was twitching and he let out a roar of laughter: 'Christ, what a party!' he said. 'Aren't any of you buggers going to offer me a bottle of beer?'

11 ❧ *All Fall Down*

'Whom Fortune wishes to destroy she first makes mad', observed Publilius Syrus and hubris, from which I had begun to suffer, is a form of madness, an insolent conviction of superiority, a wilful blindness in a country where every other man can see. I think it was Oak's decision to offer me further employment that brought on this dangerous state of mind.

Two days after the fire he sent for me. He had set aside his party mood. 'I'll give you more work', he said abruptly, 'but only if you clean up the mess you've made. And at your expense. You must have the burnt logs cut back to smaller sizes, and I intend to reduce the felling rate for the trees still standing. Your men will have to load my lorries and I'll only give you half the normal price for that. My sawmillers ask more for dirty wood and I can't see why I should be at the losing end. But first, be honest, can you afford to go on? If not, I'll call it a day.'

'Yes', I said, 'only just. But I can.'

It was true that after I had paid extra money for the fire fighting, settled claims for burnt clothing and the cost of five gallons of best beer, laid out for the re-cutting of logs, and subsidised the loading of the lorries I would still be in pocket. If I could thus overcome a major setback how wonderfully well I would do in normal circumstances!

I was obsessed with the idea of expansion. Timber contractors remained in great demand and additional contracts were not hard to find. I wrote to every timber merchant within a hundred-mile radius and the response was excellent.

Having cleaned up at Moy, Bob took Dobbin, Charlie and our six men to a hutted camp, provided by Oak, at the foot of a precipice bristling with pine. I left Bob in charge and spent my days driving to a number of places where I set up cutting contracts using local labour. I only offered for those jobs where the timber could be left in the wood. Within a few months I was employing seven contractors and my bank manager had readjusted his manner to 'warm', for the sums I was now pushing casually across his counter bore no more resemblance to my former best offerings than do fleas to elephants. As soon as a new job was set up I went hot-foot for another, snatching brief nights at the Bungalow to tell an astonished Joan that a new tycoon had been born.

If it were so he didn't live long. In the end he was to go the way of the mushroom magnate and the prince of poultry. A place called Glen Fiddich (a name ennobled by whisky) was my Wall Street (when it crashed).

I went there, looking for a contractor named McCabe, on a damp November evening of the same year. It is a narrow gut of a valley furnished by a squat, grey stone shooting lodge. Its north bank is steeply seamed by narrow gullies and at that time a forest of mixed conifers had been badly blown about by the hurricane and formed a random pattern of tumbled wood. I did not like the look of it. The price would have to be good.

As I drove up the glen a thick mist was creeping down the slopes. It would be hard to inspect the place in the failing light. McCabe was a sub-contractor who had horses but no labour to cut the trees. On the face of it an arrangement between us might work but I always preferred direct negotiation with the merchant who had bought the timber. I had few illusions about contractors: many of them were men of straw who would promise you an earth they did not own. The further I drove the less I liked the idea. There was no sign of McCabe's wooden caravan and suddenly I did not want to find it. I had better things on my plate than this. I was under no obligation to the man and was on the point of turning for home when I saw the caravan. The contractor stood beside it, removing the collar from a large horse. He saw me and gave a surly wave. It was too late to turn back.

McCabe was a tall man who had once been handsome. He was very dirty and had shifty eyes. But the horse I had seen and another that was grazing nearby were fine, sturdy beasts and their equipment, stacked against the caravan, looked serviceable. I suggested to McCabe that we examined the wood while there was light in the sky. 'Ach, no', he said, 'will ye no' tak' a dram wi' me first?' I replied that I would prefer to postpone the pleasure until we had something to talk about; he agreed and we stumbled up the rough face of the hill. There were some fine big pine up there lying amidst a tangled mass of smaller woods, thorns and whin-bushes. It would be absolute hell to take out but that was not my problem. If I could get a good price from him we could make something of it. We rumbled down the hill on a shifting bed of scree and entered McCabe's dwelling.

It was horrible. The look of the man should have prepared me for it. There was a nauseating smell of bacon fat, whisky, wood smoke, paraffin, unwashed clothes and sweat. The light from two shrunken candles showed a straw-filled bunk, a shelf supporting empty bottles, a brace of cracked cups, and plates unscoured since their day of purchase. The floor was carpeted by tattered sacks. I wondered why I was wasting my time. I would get no money from this man, but I had to hear him out.

He repeated the offer of a whisky. I felt I needed it to settle my stomach against the stench but how was I to drink it? McCabe, to do him justice, saw my problem. 'Tak' watter?' he asked, gesturing towards a bucket that was probably shared by the horses. 'Oh no', I answered, 'as it comes.' 'Ah weel, guid man, we'll crack a halfie each.' He rummaged beneath a blanket and extracted two halves of the very best Malt. 'Yon's yours. Have to hide't from the loon, thieving braat.' He spun the stopper and tipped a big mouthful down his throat. I did the same and shortly felt better.

Half an hour later our business was finished. We had made some sort of arrangement. McCabe had been honest with me. He told me that he had once been a sawmiller – a claim supported by the grisly absence of four fingers on his right hand – but that he had been 'bad with his chest' and

had spent some months in hospital. During that time his wife
– 'yon bitch' as he referred to her – had cleared off, and he
had taken to the drink. Next he lost his fingers and that put
paid to the sawmilling so he bought two horses. He couldn't
always work, his chest still troubled him from time to time;
but the loon was good and strong. 'Where is the loon now?'
I asked, for I had seen only McCabe. 'Doon beneath the
van', he answered. 'I made a wee shelter. A man's got to
have his privacy, and I canny keep drink aboot when yon's
around. It'd tak' it when I slept.' I looked shocked. 'Do you
mean he's out in the open in this cold weather?' He grinned
at me as though I had made a joke. 'He's? Oh, times;
sometimes I let 'im in. Depends. You dinny think he's deed
and buried?' He banged on the floor and shouted: 'Jochan,
Jochan, com ben the hoose, the maan wants tae see yer!'

I didn't really want that, but it was nice to know the
creature was extant. A few seconds later the door of the
cabin opened and Jochan entered the caravan. I was surprised to see that the loon was unmistakably female. She
also looked quite comely beneath her grime. Swelling the
coarse overalls at chest level were two shapely bulges and
her wide hips had a fecund look about them. But she was
certainly a very big and strong girl who could handle horses
and that was all that concerned me.

As we talked the horse-girl sat silently on a bench drinking whisky out of a cup. McCabe explained the current
situation. He had been offered a fine price to bring down the
timber and sure, he would see me right too. I put a good
price to him and he accepted without haggling. He must, I
concluded, be doing very well. He pointed out that my
payment would come with his when the logs were measured
at the roadside. This was normal. He claimed that his two
horses could keep six men busy: I doubted that and agreed
to send four. He grinned again.

After this I left. I shook McCabe's mangled hand and
nodded to the horsegirl. She still sat on the bench, saying
nothing. Her eyes were very big and bright. I had to drive
some distance up the glen before I could find a place to

turn. On my way past the caravan I remembered my anorak – I had left it on a bench. As I was about to tap on the door I became aware of a rhythmic sound and the rustle of straw, punctuated at intervals by grunts and gasps. Oh well, I thought, turning away, damn the anorak. Poor people, it's a pretty miserable life. I'm glad they're able to get some pleasure out of it.

I heard from McCabe a few days later. In a grubby note he told me the timber merchant who employed him was sending two bothies to the glen that afternoon. Bob agreed to take four cutters from the Brin job where cutting was outpacing the horse. They left by bus for Dufftown from which point McCabe had promised to pick them up in his lorry. I hadn't seen this vehicle which, when I had visited him, had been under repairs in a Dufftown garage. I was now rather suspicious. Considering his circumstances McCabe seemed to manage eventualities rather too well: his ready acceptance of a high price, his boastful attitude towards his horses and the happy coincidence of a lorry serviced and ready on just the right day all made me uneasy.

I was more so when Bob telephoned me from Dufftown two days later. Bob did not use the telephone lightly. It meant trouble. His first words 'The bugger's flitted', followed by, 'It's stone mad up here', prepared me for a picture that he traced out for me later. They had arrived at the Dufftown garage to find no lorry, nor had the owner ever heard of McCabe. At this news Bob had been in a quandary. His instinct was to get the earliest bus home until he remembered that all the other contracts were fully manned and his four men would be redundant elsewhere. He decided to trust to luck and make for Glen Fiddich, so hired a van from the garage owner.

Bob had been quite surprised to find McCabe and his horse-girl still in the area. He came across them lying beneath an old lorry trying to fit a half-shaft. McCabe was free with apologies but failed to make up a good story. Only one of the bothies had arrived and it was just large enough to accommodate two men. This upset the squad but McCabe, with the open-handedness I had experienced, drew two bottles of Malt from his store and later everybody bedded down as best they could like a tinful of drunken sardines.

It was a different mood in the morning. There were a few sore heads, no cooking equipment, and Bob was not sure what to do. He had no faith at all in McCabe and was sure that no work his men might do there would be paid for. He went to see McCabe. The contractor had a wicked hangover. In reply to Bob's suggestion that he take his horses up to the wood to drag behind the cutters he remarked insultingly: 'Dinny bother ye ass: we'll tak' oot in an hour what ye can cut in a week.' Then he relapsed into unconsciousness. The horse-girl was up and feeding the horses but she had nothing whatever to add.

In the end they decided to start cutting. The activity made the men feel better and Bob was pleased to find some good trees, clean and straight, which would prove profitable. With better tempers they worked until dusk and then made their ways back to the camp. But there they were in for a shock. McCabe, the girl, the two horses, the lorry and the caravan had vanished as though they had never existed. Nothing was left but a pile of tins and empty bottles. A black fury filled every man but since no one fancied the ten-mile walk to Dufftown they squeezed once again into the bothy and bunked down in great disgust.

In the morning they were wakened by two policemen. One was a sergeant. He came at once to the point. 'Who's the contractor here?' he asked. Bob rose to his feet with difficulty and nodded. 'Your name?' enquired the sergeant. 'Bob Wilson', said Bob. 'Oh aye, just so', replied the policeman, clearing his throat and drawing a notebook from his pocket. He went on: 'William Morrison, also known as Duncan McCabe, also known as Robert Wilson, I am arresting you for the theft of two horses, the property of Mr John Fraser, timber merchant of Rhynie in the county of Aberdeenshire. There is a further charge, namely, that you did, on 2nd November 1953, break into and enter the premises of Arthur Watt and Sons, licensed grocers in Dufftown, county of Banff and steal therefrom two cases of whisky and one thousand cigarettes. It is my duty to warn you –'

'Hold hard', shouted Bob, 'I'm not McCabe! We came here to cut trees for a contractor in Carr Bridge – my boss, Mr Frere. McCabe or Morrison, or whatever his name is, pulled out last night. We're after his guts just as much as you are!'

'I doubt it,' murmured the sergeant drily, 'we've been chasing the beggar for weeks. I'll need a statement from you, if you don't mind, and possibly from your boss. But of course you're in the clear. As a matter of fact', he confided, 'I didn't think you could be McCabe because he never works any racket without that dumb daughter of his, but I had to go through the motions. Now I take it you chaps are stuck. If you don't mind riding in a police van we'll fit you all in and give you a lift back to Dufftown.'

'So that was that', said Bob, completing his account of the way I had been duped, 'he was a bad 'un, right enough.'

'Do you really mean to say that horse-girl was his daughter?' I asked.

'Aye, no doubt about it. She was on probation as well.'

'Would you believe it? Good God!' I said.

The debacle at Glen Fiddich properly put things out of step. It produced an imbalance in the allocation of labour. We took the four men back to Brin and very soon the face of that rugged outcrop was littered with hundreds of trees. Dobbin and Charlie, aided now by Bob, worked like coloured people but they were outnumbered by the cutters three to one and while the place was a fellers' paradise it was also a draggers' hell. On this business my outlay well exceeded my income and only the profits from three straightforward contracts over the border in Aberdeenshire kept my account in balance. And then there was the work at Gairloch, in Wester Ross.

This was the second of the two contracts Oak had offered me. He had advised me to leave it alone until Brin was completed but my expansionist plans overcame his cautious words. I had been to the place, had fallen in love with it at once and feared that if I delayed too long he might give the work to another man. Its situation was magnificent. The wood, a windblow of huge Douglas Fir and tall, sleek Silver Spruce, lay on the edge of the rocky gorge of the River Kerry, a few miles from the sea, and all around it were the high mountains of Torridon which as a youth I had known and loved. Here would be an opportunity to climb, to couple business with the keenest pleasure I knew. Without delay, all prudence cast aside by this glittering prospect, I engaged two men, housed them in one of Oak's cabins and told them to start cutting. Since Oak's firm custom was never to pay for cut timber until it reached his mill I agreed to send them weekly subsistence until a final settlement could be made. This had been before the recession which had started with Glen Fiddich and as business had then stood it was not an unreasonable arrangement. But now it was a different story.

And before that same recession we had made a grand plan for the Bungalow. We had thought about it for years but now the means to implement it were in our reach. The Bungalow's low profile and crenellated parapets may have had a kind of unusual charm but the flat roof, covered in layers of old bitumenised felt, had become so porous that we dreaded continual rain or lingering snow. We patched it, poured hot tar into the cracks and put down strips of new felt but it only made a temporary improvement. We decided we would go the whole hog and put an L-shaped low-pitched timber roof over the entire dwelling.

Joan worked out her design and I obtained estimates for the material. Good timber was now becoming available without the need for a building licence. We planned to cover the roof with green rubberised tiles. It was a great idea and our enthusiasm for it knew no bounds. Finally we had the cost worked out.

I referred to my current bank statement. 'A bit short', I remarked, 'but not too bad. Oh damn, I forgot the cost of tiling. Now that does leave rather a gap. I wonder . . .?'

'What are you wondering?' Joan was disappointed.

'Well, I must leave a few hundred in the account, in case of eventualities. Winter's coming and with bad weather I'm sure to have to put some men on time. But, look, supposing we could interest a Building Society in giving us a fifty percent loan on the house?'

'Do you think that's a good idea? I like things clean cut. We'd be tied up for years paying back interest and capital. And we could never get away from here.'

'We'll have to wait for the roof then. But don't worry, the money's coming in like water through a bung-hole. By next Spring . . .'

'No, I can see if we wait it'll never be done. Perhaps you'd better have a word with a Building Society. It's up to you. But I would like a roof soon; the damp and cold in this place is shocking.'

So I went to them and we made an agreement. They valued the Bungalow and offered sixty percent towards the cost of improvements. But these simple negotiations had taken longer than expected and the winter came sooner. By the time their cheque was in my hands there were two feet of snow above our heads and it was clear that the work would have to wait until the Spring. With unusual prudence I withdrew a forty percent share of the cost from my current account and credited it to my deposit account which I had opened with the Society's cheque. 'So you see', I said to my wife, feeling rather clever, 'when we do start work we'll have a little extra in the account from the interest and if it's an early Spring I could start building the roof by February.'

But by February there were thirty acres of cut logs waiting to be pulled down the steep face of Brin rock. Ten men, in five working couples, were sweeping their way towards the end of the heavy forest. As they moved west the ground became steeper yet, sharp cliffs and beds of scree abounded, and though this slowed them not one whit it brought

Dobbin and his attendants almost to a halt. Charlie had enlisted a strong young friend whose sole function was to manhandle the logs over the precipice but the bigger logs could only be shifted by the horse. Each day as I came to add my quota of strength, I drove over a hump of the road which allowed a panoramic view of the front of the rock. Each day, with growing misgiving, I saw the gap between fellers and horsemen grow wider. And yet there was a fortune, albeit a small one, lying out on that hill. To get my hands on it I only needed a second horse.

We had been trying to get one for over a month. There were horses aplenty in the valley but none with experience of dragging wood. I would buy or hire, I didn't mind which; but the horse would have to know its work. The devastated front of Brin rock with its hanging buttresses and treacherous bracken-covered scree was no place to take a beast who was accustomed to the shafts or the plough. To make the situation more tantalising, Jack, Charlie's pal, could handle Dobbin as well as Charlie and was keen to have a horse under his charge.

Then, having widened our enquiries, we heard of a garron at Keith. I hired it unseen and sent a horse-box for it. It was an unwise thing to do but the situation was growing more ruinous by the hour. By good chance it could have been another Dobbin but the broken-down creature that staggered down the ramp was of quite a different calibre. It was an old horse, past retiring age. It was of abnormal shape with long, spindly back legs and short front ones. On level ground its back sloped downwards, giving it the appearance of a dispirited kangaroo. When it could be persuaded to climb the hill it used its front legs like claws to pull itself up, sending down a cascade of stones and earth upon its attendant.

We put it to the test, hoping for a miracle, but the poor animal's build made it impossible for it to drag a log downhill. It seemed anxious to please, in a resigned sort of way, even to the extent of sitting on its haunches and clawing itself along. There was something very poignant in the way it would watch Dobbin's powerful and meticulous performance; the look in its sad, brown eyes was of the kind which a crippled schoolboy reserves for his hero, a rugger blue. We set it light work on gentle slopes but it had only a man's pulling power: 'Give me a collar', said Bob, 'and I'll get more down any day.'

The end came when a small log, being towed on flat ground, caught behind a stump. The horse made a feeble attempt to free it, the log came off the stump and the animal turned a complete somersault. It lay on its back, winded, its hooves still describing circles in the air.

'Bob' I said, 'it must go back to its owner. I can't stand this. It's making me cry.' He was equally affected and led the horse away to its stable. I rang the carter who had brought it but before he could come the horse had run off. No one saw it go or could say how so fragile a thing had kicked down a sturdy stable door but despite a day-long search of the woods and moorlands it was not seen again then, or ever afterwards. The owner wanted compensation. I sent him my cheque for two pounds which should have satisfied him.

The final crunch came in three neatly-timed instalments. At Brin the woodsmen had sensed that I was in difficulties. In blue and frosty weather, below the snowfalls that lay heavy on the higher hills, they made one great effort to finish and be gone. In a single week they threw three hundred trees and then the axes and the saws went silent at last. In that silence I heard the cry 'Money now.'

Bob, Charlie, Jack, Dobbin and I worked like creatures possessed to get some of it but the pace we had set was a wicked one for tired men and the horse's temper had grown short. One day, toiling on sliding scree, he kicked out and struck Charlie in the chest, knocking him over a small cliff. The boy was in great pain but still protested that he would be back in a few days, even after the doctor, to whom I had taken him, had bound up a broken collar bone. I thought that I would hardly last in business for so long and knew that Charlie's employment with me was over. So I drove him home and met his ogre father for the first time. But by then the ogre had softened into a kindly man, no longer contemptuous of a shiftless layabout but proud of a son who had taken a hard knock in a man's job. The ten pounds I added to his final wage was at first rejected on the grounds that all wages had been paid and no more was due but I claimed the privilege of friendship and in the end my gift was graciously received. It warmed my heart that was otherwise growing very cold indeed.

As I reached the Bungalow that night I found Joan engaged on our grand design. She was in a cheerful mood. 'Don't you think, darling', she said, 'that the gable should come a little further. More like this . . .' Her pencil rapidly sketched in four hundred pounds worth of roof.

'Yes', I said, 'I expect so.'

She bridled a bit. 'You don't seem very enthusiastic.'

'Sorry, I'm rather tired. It's been one of those days.' I didn't bother to tell her about Charlie.

'Well, come in and have some supper. It's ready.'

'That's nice. I think I'll have a whisky first.'

'Do that. I'll join you. By the way, there's a letter for you.'

On top of the whisky the letter gave me heart-burn. It was from the Aberdeenshire timber merchant from whom I had taken two of my contracts. It told me that heavy snow had prevented all further work in the areas and advised me that my men would not leave his bothies until I had brought their wages up to date.

So Bob and I were left alone at Brin, with Dobbin who had the heart of a Derby winner, and for three weeks we nibbled the edge of a wilderness of logs: while at home I signed away my bank balance and then did another, a bad but unavoidable thing, to slake the thirst for money. And then Oak came in a mighty rage, saying he wanted wood at his mill not lying on a blasted hillside, and that he wanted it *now*. 'Have some sense man', he shouted at me, 'you'll kill the horse and yourselves. You've taken on too much. At this rate the stuff'll be rotten before this hill is cleared.' He went on to say that he would relieve me of the work and would send in a strong team of men and horses: but because the remaining timber was in the worst places it would cost him twice as much. 'And that means', he said, 'that you won't have much left to come.'

I had only just stopped reeling when he delivered the final broadside. 'You'd better get over to Gairloch', he remarked as he climbed into his white Jaguar. 'I walked over that wood the other day and spoke to one of your men. They've done a good job but they're moaning like hell. Chap I saw said he hadn't heard from you for a fortnight and swore you owed them about three hundred pounds. If you don't go and do something about that you'll really be in the shit.' Oak was not a swearing man, so that carried conviction. Nor had I reason to doubt the sum. I was only surprised to find it didn't seem to matter much.

On my way home I called into a public house. I am not given to solitary drinking but, beset by problems as I was, my judgement and my courage were both impaired. When I was fit to drive again I carried on. As I turned up the Station Road I noticed that it had been raining all day. That was not going to help. As I expected my wife's first words were, 'When are we going to do something about this roof? The chintz cover on Richard's bed is ruined by filthy tarry water. Now you promised me you'd start to build in February. It's nearly April and nothing's done. Well?'

I had collapsed into a chair. 'Come and sit on my lap', I said, 'and I'll tell you a story.' I felt secure behind a film of alcohol and ready to give full tongue to my sins.

'Why?' she asked, and added uncertainly, 'Have you been drinking?'

'Oh yes.'

She regarded me narrowly.

'Come here', I repeated, 'and sit on my lap. You look nice this evening.'

'Do I?' she said, cautiously advancing.

When she was seated comfortably I went on in verse:

'If you lack hope, ideas and intuition
And energy and grit to get things done
One thing alone can save you from perdition
And that is suicide, my son.'

She wriggled free and got up. 'That proves it – you *have* been drinking. What's this nonsense poem got to do with anything?'

'I'll tell you. Bring me a small whisky and twenty cigarettes. In about ten minutes I'll be mellow enough to make a full confession.'

'No more whisky. What are you talking about? I know your contracts haven't been going well. You've bored me to death about it for weeks. So what is it?'

I braced myself. 'No contracts, no money and no roof. Or rather one contract left. That's at Gairloch. But I owe hundreds of pounds to the men there, or so I'm told.'

'Oh lord. But what's this to do with the roof money?'

'I spent every red cent of it in getting clear of the other jobs.'

'You did *what?*'

'Spent it all. I had to, there wasn't any choice. It was a combination of most evil chances. My boat just didn't come in.'

'How are we going to repay the building society?'

'I've no idea. But of course I do have money owing to me from some of these jobs. It's probably not as bad as it seems.'

'That's all right then.' She came over and gave me a kiss. 'Don't worry about it. The children are all right and we'll manage somehow. We always have done. Put on the kettle, I'll make some supper and we'll go to bed early. In the morning we can decide what to do.'

12 ❧ *The Cabin on the Kerry*

'Don't you think', I said to Bob, 'they might have put it in a less exposed place?' It was about three weeks after I had made my admission to Joan and my man and I were seated in John Oak's cabin – a wooden shed built on the chassis of an old lorry – on the edge of a vertical drop into the River Kerry, three miles from Gairloch. It was a night of streaming West Coast rain and the wind was flatulent. Each time it burped the cabin rocked and seemed to edge nearer to the precipice. Far below us the flood waters rushed and jostled through a narrow gap.

'It's OK,' answered my friend, 'it's on hard rock. You'll see in the morning. I was asking, did Mrs Frere and Master Teddy go down to England?' I had only just joined him and he was anxious for news.

'Yes, they did. On the afternoon train from Inverness. I couldn't really leave them alone at the Bungalow. If you'd been there, it'd have been different – it needs a man about the house. And then, you know, there's the money problem.' Bob had been told something about that, but not all. I was sensitive about the enormity of my mismanagement. My mother also had been kept in the dark, for had she known the true situation she would have demanded that Joan and Richard stay with her. Logically it would have been a sensible thing but theirs was a volcanic relationship which might erupt at any time and it was better that Joan accept a long-standing invitation to stay with friends in Cambridge. That morning we had shut up the little house and left it vacant for the first time in five years. To me, at least, it was a poignant moment. It had become a creation of Joan's art and the sweat of my brow and in that it was like having made a child. As things stood there was no telling when, or even if, we should live in it again. This mood of uncertainty stayed with me to the very moment I kissed my wife and son goodbye on Inverness station. It was less like seeing one's family off on holiday than a farewell on the scaffold. I had been very low in spirits when I started to drive West but my mood improved as I considered the challenge ahead. Bob and I were going to work this last remaining contract between us and we were going to make it a success.

'Did you find the men?' I enquired. He had come here, with Dobbin, a week earlier and I had given him all the spare money I could rake up to settle with the woodcutters.

'Aye, in the end, I did that. And paid 'em right up. I gave 'em twenty pound apiece.'

'What! They were content with that?'

'Didn't ask for more. And I didn't offer it. Reckon they've found a better way of making the spondulicks.'

'They have? Is there something they know which I don't?'

'Aye, seems there's pearls in this here creek. When this spate's over they'll find plenty. And there's a craft shop in the village that makes Celtic jewellery. No trouble at all.'

'But they've cut some trees, surely. John Oak said they had.'

'Sure, they do that too. A fair puckle trees. Enough to keep us dragging for a month. But they aren't greedy. Of course they've got the cable too.'

'What cable?'

'An old wartime thing. Belonged to the Post Office, they think. It runs through the wood and is about a mile long. Thick as your arm.'

'I don't see –'

'But they did', Bob grinned. 'The lads are right well organised. When the river's high and no good for pearls, and the weather's too wet for cutting they take bits off the cable and melt it down. It's pure copper. There's a bloke on a regular fish run and he sells it to scrappies in Aberdeen. He gets a bit for his trouble and they're making a bomb. Won't think of moving on until they've cleaned up the lot, and they're only on the first hundred yards. Pair of thieving

Newfies, of course', Bob ended, on a note of admiration.

'What enterprise!' I said, 'and they'll go on cutting for us?'

'Aye, sure. They're kind of grateful to have the accommodation, like. I saved most of your money.' He showed me a bundle of notes of encouraging thickness.

'Why, Bob, that's marvellous. It'll give us a start . . . Oh, my God, what's that?'

One end of the cabin had seemed to rise a little from the ground. It shook violently. 'Hold on to that money', I shouted, 'and let's get out of here. The thing's going into the river.'

Bob gave me a grin. He didn't move. 'Reckon it's Dobbin', he said composedly. 'He grazes evenings on the side of the road. When he's ready for bed and oats he puts his shoulder to the cabin. It's his way of telling me he's back. I'll just take him up to the stable; it's one of Oak's on the top side of the road. You won't have seen it in the dark. When I come back we'll have a cuppa and a tin of strew.'

I was beginning to enjoy myself. 'Ask him if he wouldn't mind pushing from the other side', I said, 'it's safer that way.'

Bob had scrubbed out the cabin and had made it very cosy. He had prepared my bed by collecting a quantity of dry bracken and laying it on the slats of one of the fixed bunks. A cauldron of boiling water for washing, stood on top of the red-bellied woodsman's stove, the heat from which had raised the temperature to tropical levels. We had the Tilley lamps we had once used in the Bungalow. After a satisfying meal, I finally went to sleep and dreamt that I was in the mountain hut on Ben Nevis. And when I woke it was with the same keen sense of anticipation that I had been accustomed to feel in those far off days.

'I'll make some grub', said Bob, from the opposite bunk, 'while you take a walk through the wood. Then we can talk about it while we eat.' I dressed in front of the stove – the very epitome of degenerate comfort – and went out into the morning. Directly beneath my feet the River Kerry growled like a long dog and over its surly voice innumerable wood pigeons cried in the Silver Fir. The rain had stopped but a gossamer mist, rose pink in front of the rising sun, was laced around the highest trees. The sky was a gentle blue and the air was as soft as a kind kiss. It was the sort of morning that demanded to be walked in and I determined that after examining the work I would carry on to the nearest high point and look for the big mountains which I had once known so well. 'Give me about an hour, Bob', I called back to him, 'there's a lot to see.'

And the first thing was the hydro-electric pipe. You couldn't help seeing it where it ran like a vast green snake of steel between the fallen timber and the road. For most of its length it must prove an insuperable barrier to the horse; it was five feet across and stood two feet from the ground on concrete supports. But for thirty yards or so it lay in a cutting and here it could be bridged. I saw that Bob had not been slow in taking the point. On the bank two trees, as straight as telegraph poles, had been drawn into position and there were a pile of short lengths and coils of fencing wire.

In the dispersing mist the windblows looked enormous. I wondered if Dobbin would ever be able to pull their cut sections to the road. Though the horse never failed to surprise me there must be a limit to what he could do. And there was a bridge yet to be built. There was a comfort in knowing that the Newfies had been working further down the valley where there was no pipe to impede our progress. The cash flow would start there. But this place, which contained the bulk of the timber, would have to be tackled, and sooner rather than later, for Oak had no patience with a man who skimmed the cream from the milk. He was quite likely to dismiss me from the job if he suspected that I was going to leave him with the whey.

Well, we should see. Bob and I would soon discuss it and few things daunted Bob. Brushing aside my misgivings I climbed steadily through the trailing mist until the wood was far behind me. Mushy heather slopes, furrowed by eroded peat bogs, terminated in a thin ridge of rock which wore a cairn like a comic hat. I sat down beside it, breathing deeply. Yes, they were all there, my old friends. Baosbheinn, like a grey battleship aground on his moor, Beinn Eighe of the quartzite comb and tumbled, red-brown terraces, Liagach's tent-shaped summit and dependant pinnacles and squat monstrous Slioch frowning down on Loch Maree's faery islands. Each of them held a special memory for me, each of them was a huge reminder of some of the best days of my life. Thus glorified and freed from common care I waited awhile until the growing sun warmed my cheeks and I remembered that I was a straw-man, dispossessed by my own folly of wife and children, exiled from my home. Much was needed from me before I might indulge myself. I sighed and made my way back down the hill to Bob and breakfast.

Bacon and eggs, toast, with or without marmalade, and hot sweet tea were on the menu when I reached the cabin and Dobbin, having his private guzzle, gave me a look which plainly said: 'You're late for work.' But by evening he was glad enough to call a halt for we had driven him hard. Bob had seen the bridge as an absolute priority and before sundown it was in use. It consisted of three strong trunks in line with innumerable cross members wired into the structure. It spanned about thirty feet, just clearing the pipe. To begin with Dobbin distrusted it flatly. He would not risk a hoof upon it. It was fortunate that when we invited him to cross it he was on the top side of the pipe, having been led there via the Newfies' preserve where the pipe ended. Therefore the bridge lay between him and his oats and hay and he was a hungry horse. At five o'clock, his regular feed time, he was still pawing the first round log of the bridge. 'Right', said Bob, who always addressed Dobbin in recalcitrant mood, as though he were a youngest brother, 'if you won't cross, no grub tonight. You'd hardly expect me to bring your oats up here, now would you? But it'll be ready, as usual, at the cabin. It's up to you.'

The performance which then took place must lose much in the telling. As soon as we were half-way back to the cabin, a matter of fifty yards, Bob said to me: 'You must watch this. That beast is half human.' We crouched down in a hollow where we were invisible to Dobbin but could see him clearly. For a good five minutes he made no move, then very cautiously he shuffled his front hooves onto the bridge, tested it and then moved forward step by cautious step until he was on the other end. I was about to spring up and shout 'Bravo' when Bob laid a restraining hand on my shoulder: 'Wait you', he said, 'you ain't seen nothin' yet.' Dobbin turned on his hooves and went back the way he had come with a confident swagger until he stood again exactly where we had left him. Then he threw back his head and whinnied at the top of his voice. Bob motioned me to rise: 'Let's give him a big hand', he said. We clapped and cheered loudly while the horse, throwing caution to the winds, sprang onto the suspended timbers and thundered across. Bits of bark and some turf we had stuffed between the logs flew out behind him. He went by us with his head in the air and did not stop until he reached his feeding place beside the cabin. 'Good grief', I said in amazement, 'he's an exhibitionist. This isn't ordinary. It's exactly what *I* would have done in the same circumstances.'

Several months went by. Bob and I, with nothing to do but work, eat and sleep, filled the unforgiving minute to the brim and made great inroads into the fallen timber. We rotated the work programme on a three-day basis, taking out the Newfies' timber, cutting our own, and then extracting it. Dobbin rested on the second day. Twice a week Oak's lorry, driven by a giant gem of a man named Johnny Roy, came and relieved us of our produce and brought feed for the horse. With hardly any overheads, personal or business, my battered finances took another turn for the better. I enjoyed the work and was enormously fit. In these conditions it is easy not to worry: just being alive is sufficient. It has always been my contention that if all the nations' leaders were practising athletes there would be little fear of war.

By the end of June, however, two problems began to

loom up like rocks in the smooth sea of pleasant day to day existence. One concerned the work. The Newfies had melted down the last of the cable and in the dry weather the Kerry's yield of pearls was low. They had also done as much cutting as they could for they used small bushman saws rather than a single two-man crosscut and many trees were too large for them. So they said a cheerful farewell and set off to the city to become scrap merchants. Bob and I were left wondering how to maintain our output.

We found the answer in the *Exchange & Mart*. It was one of the new petrol-driven chain saws, a Danarm. It was a mechanical animal with a ferocious bite. It came on the bus from Inverness, early one morning. By evening it had done the work of four men. That was one problem solved.

The other concerned my family. Joan and Richard were happy with our friends as was Heather at school, but it was not a situation which could go on indefinitely. Guests are guests, and children have school holidays. Also it was high time to resume married life. Since Bob and I were a two-man band playing a score which would still last many months I could not leave him and return to Carr Bridge. With Heather's holidays beginning in early July it was clear that I must rent a house in the district. It would be an ideal solution if such a place could be found. I knew that it would suit Joan for she loves the sea and the warmth and wetness of the west.

Unexpectedly a house was not hard to find. It came to light at Badachro, a small fishing village five miles from the Kerry on the south shore of Loch Gairloch. Lochside Farm, a low building with an air of severity, was owned by Mrs Wilhelmina Fraser and her husband Robert. They were dark, quiet people who lived in great fear of God in their dark, quiet house. Especially on Sundays. At Badachro the whole week was rather subdued by the inevitability of the seventh day. I had heard the tale of the two men of the coast who were discussing, rather morbidly, where and when they would prefer to die. One said: 'At my own fireside on a Friday night, for 'tis payday and the drams would be in me.' But the other shook his head: 'Na, na, Andrew, I would be for passing away in Badachro on a Sunday.'

'On Sunday, in Badachro, Hamish? Why so, man?'

'Cos then I wouldn'a notice the transition.'

There was truth in that, but the Frasers were pleasant folk, nonetheless, and the situation was a dream. There is a miniature bay, enclosing a tidal island, a tiny pub and jetty, and behind it the empty moors gather themselves up to the jagged ridges of Torridon. All around, night and day, are the sea sounds; gulls scavenge on the shore or beat the air with powerful wings, and the sluicing water rises and falls through coarse rock pools festooned with multicoloured seaweeds. Loch Badachro lies behind the farm, an appendix shape within a fringe of stunted oak scrub, and sends its peaty waters to the sea through a short, rocky channel with steep sides.

'So that's the bridge we built, and here's our cabin' I said to Joan and my son, as the Fraser Nash crunched to a halt outside it a week later. How good it was to see them! For days I had been imagining the moment when the train came in, the kiss of greeting from my wife, my son's excited face. It had been just as I had planned it. My mother had been pleased to see us too but sent us away with boxes of provisions, as though we were poor relations, to keep us free from want in the days to come. Over all the sun grinned down deliriously from a fat, round, June sky: the day had started wonderfully well.

We halted at the cabin, shouting for Bob. Soon he appeared in the distance, riding Dobbin down the slope. There was another round of greetings: 'Holy Old Smoke, Mistress Frere, you're looking grand. Master Teddy, how'se about a bit o' dorg rough?' Richard settled for a ride on Dobbin up to the bridge. In their brief absence my wife and I acknowledged our reunion with renewed warmth.

From the moment of their meeting, an hour later, Joan got on well with Mrs Wilhelmina Fraser. I had been afraid that my wife's sunny and cheerful temperament would clash with the other's 'we die tomorrow and must be prepared' attitude, a tribal memory of surly John Knox. But her response was quite different. Later, when we had settled in a bit, she said to me: 'This is a nice place, much better than Carr Bridge. I do hope we can stay. Mrs Fraser says there's a little school in the village where Richard could go. That would solve a problem. You do remember he's five now, don't you?' I hadn't actually forgotten though the educational implications of the fact had been obscured by my concentration on the means of survival. 'There hasn't been much time', I said defensively, 'to think about it. I've been working damned hard –'

'And having the time of your life', she added cheerfully. 'I've never seen you look so fit. But, coming back to Richard, this is just the right start. He'll have to go to prep. school next year. Now, where are you off to?'

'Back to the grind. We've two tons of logs to get on the bank before John Oak's lorry comes tomorrow. Men must work, you know, and women –'

'No', she said, 'this is one place where I won't be weeping. You'll be back for supper, or is it high tea?'

'High tea, I expect. Yes, I'll be back. And then we'll all have a nice evening. Maybe a walk on the shore.'

'Leave that one for Johnny Roy,' I said to Bob later, 'he's such a long man.' We were trying to manhandle a heavy log to the top of the pile.

'Aye' answered Bob, 'as long as I can remember! But we'll need to give him a hand. You'll be down for the loading?'

'Of course. Just because I'm living out – as they used to say in the RAF – I'm not neglecting the work. Look, there's a man just got out of his car down there. He's waving. Do you think he wants a job? I'd better go and see.'

I ran down to the road. While I was still running the man, whom I had seen about the place, shouted up at me: 'Is it yourself, Mr Frere? Your wife is wanting you to come to Fraser's farm. Your son's gone missing.'

'Missing?' I did not take it in.

'Aye, he's wandered awa' on the muir. He'll no be far, I'm thinking.' He climbed back into his car and drove off up the Kerry. I went back to Bob. My mouth had become quite dry and my legs were unsteady. 'I can't understand it but he's saying that Richard is lost. Mrs Frere wouldn't send for me unless she's worried. I must go immediately, I think.'

Bob's cheerful nature made him look younger than he was. In shock the hidden years stood out and crinkled his face like the grain on wood. Suddenly he looked very old indeed. 'Let me know when he's found', he said, 'if it's possible. If I don't hear I'll walk over as soon as the horse is bedded.'

I sprang into my car. My stomach was tight with fear, for I could not reduce the situation into harmless terms. Joan never panicked. Before she sent for me there must have been a full search. But a search of what? The small house, a couple of barns, the shaven moor on which anything bigger than a rabbit would have been visible. There remained only the loch and – oh God! – the river, churning and crushing its way between high stone banks. Momentarily I closed my eyes and the big car, travelling at speed, struck a pothole, nearly throwing me out of my seat. Above the howl of the engine my imagination supplied the high note of a child's scream gurgling into silence as black water took the place of living air.

I crashed the car to a halt outside the farmhouse. Joan, white as death, met me at the door. There was nothing to add to what the man had told me. Richard had vanished from the face of the earth. One moment he had been there, five minutes later he was gone. Mrs Fraser and Joan had searched every inch of the house, gone through the barns with a tooth comb. Fraser had called out his neighbours and several men were encircling the moor. The three of us went outside and shouted 'Richard, Richard!' at the top of our voices. Nothing stirred, nothing answered: in the warm June air there was no wind to carry away the sound, the silence was intense. It was as though every bird and beast on that empty plain, every fish in the dark loch, were holding their breaths in sympathy.

A man came up to me and said: 'I'm thinking, we must try the river.' He was quiet and apologetic as though he regretted the need to introduce the ultimate spectre. I nodded, 'I'll take the near bank.' Three men jumped down into the gorge and scrambled up the other side. I moved away, down stream, towards the sea. My mind seemed unable to lock on to the fact: it could not be happening. And then a wave of intense misery came back and I knew it was. Richard, the son of whom I was so proud, the boy Joan doted on, was no longer anywhere in the world. A brief two hours before, he had been riding behind Bob on Dobbin, laughing his head off, looking forward to his exploration of an exciting new world. And now he was . . . my thoughts checked. My blood froze. Down beneath an overhanging rock, a few feet above the water, there was a patch of blood and an arm, bent and crooked. The rest was hidden behind a twisted tree, but I knew what I should find, as we had once found another, a grown man, in the Cuillins of Skye, years before. Imprinted over present vision was that earlier one, the rag-doll figure, the dark red rose of matted hair behind the skull, the stained and sticky rock, the open, squinted eyes.

I could only drag myself to the arm and the blood. Now that my tears were flowing freely it was moments before I found only a stick and a patch of lurid lichen that leered at me from the grey rock. 'Oh God, so many thanks', I cried, acknowledging a hint of mercy. And then I went back to my search.

For a quarter of an hour I scoured the bed of the stream. In the absence of proof here there seemed to be some hope. Quite suddenly a new idea came to me – I wondered why I had not thought of it at once. Richard might have wandered down the road and been picked up by a car. He was a shy chap and a driver would not have got much sense out of him. He'd have been taken to the police station. Of course that was what had happened. I had to tell Joan at once.

I scrambled out of the river. Higher up, beyond where I had started my search, I saw the three men, now standing together. As my head and shoulders rose above the bank I heard a shout. There was something in that high urgent cry that contained a declaration, be it good or bad. 'What, what, what?' I shouted but the echoes battered the cliffs around me and made it impossible to hear. Again came the shout but this time it tangled with the bleat of a sheep that scuttled in the heather by my side. 'Shut up', I screamed, and when all the echoes had died away I heard it clear:

'The boy's drowned.'

I had known it all along. I had long indulged myself and this was my reward. My reward, and innocent Joan's.

Seeing me stand as motionless as a rock one of the men had broken away from the group and was once again recrossing the gorge. I watched his wild approach with a kind of detached interest. It didn't matter if he came or went, yet I wondered why he climbed the shale so desperately since there was nothing left to say.

He was a young black-haired Celt, and when he reached me he was quite out of breath. For a moment he stood in front of me, his shoulders heaving. His face was rustic, his expression unformed but in his dark eyes was compassion and an understanding of tragedy to which his ancient race was no stranger. He came to the point as quickly as good manners would permit.

'Good day to you. I thought you had not heard what my father was saying, for the river's loud and the rock takes the sound away.'

'I heard, my son is drowned.'

'Not *drowned*. Oh, for heaven's sake, he's *found*. He was hiding behind a wardrobe in the bedroom. I thought when I saw you stand that you couldn't have heard my father right.'

The river suddenly seemed very far away. Its raucous voice had become a distant whisper. As in another world I heard his voice, speaking the English which was not his tongue with a foreigner's care and dignity: 'Allow me to assist you. You are not well. It is the shock. Give me your arm and I will help you back to your wife and son.'

13 ❧ *The Glorious Summer*

'So that's all settled', said Chiefy Wilson. 'You pay my rates and see the electricity and telephones right, and I wish you joy of the place. It isn't hard to run, as you can see. Only mind my little robin. My wife found him in a junk shop in the Smoke and took a fancy to him. She was asking me about him only the other day. He's in a nick in the wall beside the gate. Been in lots of nicks in lots of walls round houses we lived in, and I built most of 'em.'

'Where's your wife now', asked Joan, 'on holiday?'

'You could say that,' said the builder, 'it's one way of putting it. Matter of fact she's been dead eight years. But we still keep in touch, pretty close in touch.'

'Oh, I'm so sorry', murmured Joan, 'I shouldn't . . .'

'Nonsense. Why not ask? I get a bit lonely now and then but after all it's only for a few years. And it's pretty good on the other side, so I'm told. Now look, how about you young people drinking a glass of whisky with me before you go back to Badachro? And, if you could spare the time, what do you say to a game of Monopoly?'

'We'd love to.' We owed him much more than our company for he had just agreed to let us occupy his trim bungalow on the shore at Gairloch entirely rent free. Chiefy had built Meyrick a few years earlier. It was like himself, small, solid and dependable. A Londoner by birth he had been in the private building line for years. As we grew to know him better we were to learn that apart from making houses, drinking, smoking and playing Monopoly he had a single obsession. As he said to us once: 'Building's me trade – sometimes we have to knock down a wall or two. I reckon Jeanne', his wife had been, or was, French, 'and I have knocked down the biggest wall of all.'

Joan had met this faithful man in her search for an alternative to Lochside Farm. Mrs Fraser had entertained us for five months and would have gone on doing so had she not required her rooms for visiting relatives from Canada. Our deadline for moving was a week before Christmas and we were sad at the prospect of leaving Badachro. That single harrowing day when our son went missing had been a prologue to a period of calm and earnest life, as unhurried as the long, windless autumn in which it was spent. Our work at the wood had settled down to a steady rhythm. Mechanisation here had been an unmixed blessing; the petrol chain saw severed trees from their roots as a sharp knife slices pineapple. It made it possible for us to curtail our working week from one of seven days and nearly ninety active hours to something less exacting. We had our weekends free and each day ended at six o'clock.

Joan went on enjoying Badachro: its texture suited her. And our son, placed under the care of the indomitable Miss McIntosh, the female dominie of Badachro's eight-pupil school, had a solid grounding in the four R's – religion making up the score – and a taste of such rigid discipline as has long since vanished in our sloppy and permissive society. Perhaps it might be said that here was a little too much Isaiah and too little Matthew but as starters on the menu of life this education could not be faulted. Richard respected his mistress, he went in abject fear of her and of the jealous God who stood so closely by her shoulder: but he learned.

We were to see something of this intolerant and angry deity – or at least of his influence, too long imposed, upon the tribal mind – when we moved, as a temporary expedient, into a rented house hard by Lochside Farm. There was a time gap in our accommodation plans: a fortnight between exit from Lochside and entry into Chiefy Wilson's bungalow. This place stood on a raft of solid ground encircled by black peat bog and lay on a north-facing slope which protected it, in winter, from any sun at all.

Joan and I have individual tastes and have been known to disagree about many things but concerning this house we had but a single thought: it was utterly depressing. When the four of us – Heather had just joined us for her Christmas holidays, poor child – approached the door and saw the flaked brown paint and two dead rowans on either side our spirits began to sag. We unlocked the door with a struggle – damp had seized up the mechanism – and entered doubtfully in single file. There was a smell of long-lost cabbages coupled with a strong hint of dead mice. Though outside it wanted four hours to twilight it was already mid-night within: thick curtains of some pallid stuff excluded light and air. We drew them, producing a fall-out of dust, and surveyed the interior with lack-lustre eyes.

The parlour, or front room, in which we found ourselves was stuffed with joyless Victorian furniture overlaid by utility George V. The carpet was as scuffed as an old dog and the brown wallpaper was figured and embossed by damp. Hanging high on the walls, from where they could get the most critical view, were faded photographs of Pharisees with spatulate beards and dense, mossy sideboards. Their expressions were so baleful and filled with condemnation-without-trial, so lacking in any hint of Christian charity, that Joan turned their faces to the wall.

Upstairs were two bedrooms in the roof. We chose one and sent the children to the other, but the arrangement was impermanent. Within an hour of our first bedding down in the place they were back with us. Heather claimed the attic was haunted; she had felt fingers trailing across her face. We suspected bats but were not prepared to take any chances.

Because Christmas was only three days away we decided we had no choice but suffer it. For fear it might become bogged down we had left the car at a safe distance and carried gifts and groceries through the squelching mire. On Christmas eve I set out in heavy sleet to find a suitable tree. There were no Norway spruce within carrying distance but I found a hapless Sitka on top of a bank. I took it but its untraditional form and poor gift-bearing capacity were loudly criticised. I wondered, surely this was the least of our worries?

Christmas morning dawned bright but was soon smothered under a blanket of peevish rain. You could sense the Pharisees smirking against the wall. Joan was worn out with the effort of cooking lunch on a luke-warm stove. Some of the pans leaked. There was a burst of joy when the presents were given out. It would not have pleased the old men. How they would have driven away the kings at that other gift giving!

Bob, unable to be present because of Dobbin, had sent a big teddy bear. We decided it would be fun to go and see him. But just as we drove away a rear tyre burst. John Knox's power to deflate was as strong as ever.

In the morning Joan said: 'I'll go mad if we can't get away from here. I can't stand another day. Let's phone Chiefy and ask if there's any chance of going there sooner.' Fortunately there was a phone box not two miles away, and when the builder heard our doleful tale he reset his plans and invited us to come that very afternoon. I was just about to change the tyre when Joan ran out of the house: 'Darling, there's a smell of burning. I think the place is on fire.' 'Does that matter?' I enquired, 'as long as the children, and our bits, are out?' 'Of course they are,' she answered, 'and Richard's looking a bit sly. But seriously, don't you think you ought to look?'

I found an upstairs curtain half consumed. 'Richard's got matches', remarked his big sister snidely. I questioned him closely and he murmured something along the lines of vengeance, Sodom and Gomorrah and the need for brimstone. I was not for disputing Holy Writ and was relieved that the origin of his action was not hereditary but it was plainly desirable to bring him under the influence of a less punitive religion. Half an hour later we drove away. 'I don't ever want to speak about that horrible place again', said Joan.

In fact, it was easily forgotten. Meyrick was as different from the place of the whited sepulchre as was cheese from chalk. It was Chiefy Wilson's brain child, as the Bungalow had been ours, and it was a projection of his untroubled spirit. For he, of all men, knew where he was going, and whom he was going to meet there, and in this indifferently gilded execution chamber that is no bad thing. His sober joy had rubbed off on the house.

Our entry to Meyrick was in January. There was a short spell of wild weather, hail and wet snow which briefly dusted the headlines of north Skye, so well seen from our sitting room window, and died away before the month was done. Daffodils were tall in February; March came in like a big, bouncing lamb and went out like a jolly lion. By April we were swimming in Gairloch bay and drying ourselves in the warm sun that shone on its crescent of silver sand. The glorious summer had begun.

Bob, Dobbin and I had finished clearing up the windblow at the Kerry. By good chance our next job, a thinning of mixed conifers at a place called Flowerdale, was adjacent to Gairloch village. Bob moved in the Meyrick and Dobbin, not to be outdone, took up residence in a stall we had built for him in Chiefy Wilson's garage. It was a convenient arrangement. My Fraser Nash was now sorely troubled by lack of spares and was living on expensively rented time. Its powerful engine was as virile as ever but it had no brakes to speak of and was hard to start without the tow which Dobbin inevitably provided. If it still failed to fire we simply towed it home and used the horse to carry us and our groceries from the shop in Strath a few miles away. If he was working in the wood, Joan went. She loved Gairloch and delighted to walk by the sea in all weathers.

The thinning work paid me less well than the clearing of the windblows but our outgoings were modest and our state contented. John Oak made irregular visits to the scene of our operation. He was only moderately satisfied: 'You're just playing yourself, man', he was wont to say, 'riding about on that horse like your folks did on their estates. If you start a business you want to make it grow. It's plain enough you've plenty money of your own; the pennies I'm sending you wouldn't keep a bird in worms. And you being an educated man I'd have thought by now you'd have been buying me out!' John Oak was always a man for his joke.

That long summer was a glowing background to a fresh outcrop of incidents, grave and gay, none of which could be compared in importance to the development of the hydrogen bomb or the discovery of the contraceptive pill. But it is not only Beauty that is in the eye of the beholder and to persons of small stature the horizon seems very close. It started with an accident and it ended with another.

Bob, having heard so much about it, wanted to find out what I saw in rock climbing and I had promised to give him a taste of it. At the head of the Flowerdale Valley, where the big trees ended in a stunt of pine, is a perfect miniature rocky mountain, An Groban by name, not four hundred metres high but rich in slabs, ridges and gullies. I had grown to know it well, every inch of it, and had graded its climbs in order of difficulty chiefly for the benefit of my son. My grand plan for him was beginning to mature and if his fanaticism as yet hardly matched my own I comforted myself by remembering that at the age of six I had never climbed anything higher than an East Anglian tree. And now, here was Bob showing interest and An Groban's west ridge, of small exposure and with only a single tricky pitch, was just the place for a beginner.

Though it was barely March the birches were rosily expectant and some of the larch were green. I had chosen a bland, windless afternoon. We walked past our working site where a pile of logs were awaiting Oak's lorries and up into the rough country beyond the highest trees. An Groban stood above our heads like a clenched fist. 'I'll not be getting up yon', remarked Bob gloomily, 'it'd be easier to climb a prison wall!'

I tied him on to the rope and climbed away with the ease of long acquaintance. Bob followed, testing each hold in intense concentration. It was plain that once he had the feel of the thing he was going to enjoy himself. 'You're doing fine', I said, 'it's no trouble at all to you. Just look down at the tops of our trees, see how small they are.' Bob gave them a glance but the sight didn't seem to reassure him. 'Holy

Old Smoke' he muttered, 'how did I get up here? I'll not be going down the way.' I told him that there was a little steep bit to come and then we would be on top: from there we could just walk off the hill.

We reached the little steep bit. It was no more than twenty feet high but leaned out a trifle at the top. Bob looked horror-struck. I wriggled over it and secured myself to a bollard. 'Now', I said, 'here is what you must do. When you reach the overhang there's a big block for your left foot. It's loose but quite safe to stand on, but you mustn't pull it sideways. There are plenty of other holds, and you're as safe as houses on the rope. Just watch the block.'

Bob grunted, 'Oh my gawd, what an idiot I am', and started to scramble towards me rather desperately. Just beneath the block the holds are awkwardly placed. Both feet are inserted in a narrow crack, one above the other, while the right hand grips a shallow saucer. The forbidden block with a dozen fractures ideal for support must have looked incredibly seductive, a beautiful woman whom one knows one dare not touch. When Bob's trembling feet slipped out of the crack and all the weight of his body came onto his right arm he forgot my words of warning. Before I could say: 'Don't worry, I'll lower you' his free hand snatched at the tottering stone. It rolled over, right on top of his fingers, and sailed away down to the scree where it exploded in a puff of dust.

Bob's hand was in rather a mess. He made light of it but two hours later our local doctor was quite firm: 'Two fingers are broken. It's not too serious but he'll need physiotherapy at the clinic in Inverness. It may take quite a time but the fingers will mend as good as new.'

We harnessed Dobbin and pull-started the Fraser Nash. Bob stayed in hospital that first night while I spent it at my mother's house. I told her the sorry tale. She also had a problem, having just lost her ancient maid to the creeping palsy. She asked brightly: 'If Bob has to be in Inverness for a bit, he can stay here with me. Of course I would be all right on my own' (she was both thrawn and martyr-minded) 'but he could get the cat's fish and look after Domino.' This last was a monstrous Dalmatian of wayward habits who had come from another part of the town and had never forgotten it. It was impossible to deny the sense of this arrangement but I only hoped that when Bob was restored to full activity, it might be subject to cancellation. My mother, as I knew well, had a wide wing: once under its amiable cover it was very hard to escape.

The next morning, driving west, my one hope was that I should not have a visit from John Oak. In his eyes my retrogression would have been complete: I was a one-man band at last.

Yet I was able to carry on. I had boundless energy, an efficient mechanical saw and a half-human horse. With the lengthening days I was able to put in more hours. Day after day, as March turned to April, the sun beamed down from a cloudless sky and the world turned green. I would not have exchanged my job for all the gold in South Africa. And then, without any warning, Dobbin began to fail. His deterioration was so slow that using hindsight it was impossible to mark the day of its beginning but by the end of a fortnight he was in a sorry state. He had lost all will to work, ate sparingly and stood listlessly in his stall at the Meyrick garage. A vet had promised to attend him but had been delayed by an outbreak of disease among farm animals. Three days later we opened the garage door to find Dobbin lying on the ground with a back leg extended stiffly behind him. He was grunting with pain and it did not seem as if he had very long to go.

Joan and I had examined him carefully a dozen times. Only now was the origin of his malaise made manifest. Like Napoleon's soldier boy at the siege of Ratisbon Dobbin's pride was too great to show the extent, even the nature, of his injury, and he would have died rather than allow himself the indulgence of a limp. Quickly we examined his hoof. The pastern was badly swollen and right in the centre of the pad was a gleaming steel disc a quarter of an inch across. 'Oh my God', I said to Joan, 'the poor devil.' I know my nails and this was the head of a five or six inch one: the rest of it was somewhere inside the horse's hoof.

Joan took charge at once. There is no better person in an emergency. 'It has to come out', she said, 'and now. We can't wait for the vet. Perhaps Dr Macrae . . . no, he's on holiday and we don't know his locum. Look, I'll hold the leg while you get something round the head of the nail.'

My only surgical instrument was a claw hammer. Its chief drawback was going to be the thickness of the claws. To hook the nail it would be necessary to depress the swollen flesh around it, and we could only guess what agony this would cause the horse. We both knew that there must be no fumbling or indecision. It had to succeed in one go or it would not succeed at all. 'Right', said Joan, increasing her grasp of the leg, 'do it. I'll try to hold him.'

I pressed the cold steel against the puffy, heated pad. The horse screamed shortly and drew up his leg, dragging Joan along the ground. At the same moment I hooked and pulled. The first inch of the nail came slowly, seeming to grate among bones: the remainder came out smoothly amid a burst of yellow pus which spattered our faces and clothing. There was a violent contraction of muscle, then a relaxation and Dobbin lay still: he had ceased to breathe but we could still see the great heart beating strongly in his chest. In a moment respiration returned but he made no attempt to get to his feet and when Joan applied a pad of cotton wool soaked in Dettol to the wound he hardly stirred at the contact. 'We'll leave him now', she said, 'to rest. He's a poor, tired horse. Do you think he's clear of the poison?'

I felt he must be. The concrete floor of the garage was thick with blood and pus. We had unplugged a veritable Pandora's box of germs. But I hadn't liked the way the nail had stuck, as though it were wedged in the bony tissue of the horse. I had a nasty feeling that my good friend, the only partner I had left, was going to be put out to grass.

But he confounded my fears. Within three days he was on his feet again and eating like a horse, his ribs vanished beneath a brand-new summer coat, his eyes were restored

to brightness. Before a fortnight was up he was able to
gallop to the shop to bring back a load of groceries. It was as
well for us that he could for on Friday 13th of May, a
roasting hot day, our other form of transport fell into the
sea.

We had been for a drive to Inverewe gardens, that
wonderful patch of sub-tropical paradise which a man
called Osgood Mackenzie, a horticultural visionary, had
set out a century earlier on a peaty headland. For two hours
we had wandered in the shade of the Eucalyptus trees and
admired a host of exotic plants and shrubs more usually
found in Kew Gardens and then we had come home. As she
got out of the Fraser Nash at Meyrick Joan suggested:
'Don't stop the engine. Why don't you go to the pub and
buy some cans of beer? We'll have supper outside on the
terrace.'

The pub was quite close by. It was a part of the hotel
which stood on the landward side of the main road: on the
other was a gentle grassy slope steepening to a short cliff
above the beach. I reversed off the road and parked the car
beside the pub door with the engine still running. In this,
the autumn of its life, the Fraser Nash had no hand brake: it
lacked a special cable which was impossible to get. In order
that it would stay in place I had positioned the car with one
of its back wheels in a rut. Then I went into the bar, bought
my carry-out and snatched a quick one for the road.

In those days there were only a handful of white settlers
in Gairloch and I fancy they were regarded by the local
inhabitants with a mixture of half concealed curiosity and
distrust. By now I am sure they are tolerated and sensibly
exploited, for those who enter Paradise unasked should be
made to pay the dues, but in 1955 the native people tended
to exclude the English visitor. This attitude was brought to
one's notice never more strongly than when one went into a
bar. It was manifest in the occupants' instant reversion to
the language of the Gael.

This was now the case. I was half-way through my pint
when a young man burst into the room in a state of obvious

excitement. A dramatic or an hilarious tale transcends language barriers for it is usually accompanied by gestures or mime and it was plain to me that something out of the ordinary had taken place. That it might concern me was suggested by furtive glances in my direction and the fact that the Gaelic tongue leans heavily on the English for modern words. Within a few seconds I heard 'sporting car' in a matrix of unintelligible sound and there were many slow grins and down-pointing fingers. Then the barman, almost apologetically, came over to me: 'I am sorry to say', he remarked, 'that your grey sporting car has fallen upon the beach. She ran away from where she was. And Murdo is saying that the engine is still running and the horn blowing. It is a wonderful thing indeed!'

I silently agreed and went outside, wondering, not for the first time, why bizarre mishap had made a brother of me. There was an empty space outside the bar and doleful hooting from the bottom of the slope. The car was resting with its nose in soft sand and its wheels on the rock: it was about twenty degrees from the vertical. I climbed up a few feet of cliff and turned off the ignition key through the open window. As far as I could see there was no serious injury though it was badly shaken up, but how on earth was I going to get it back on the road?

I soon had an answer to that question. Though individual response to my misfortune had been fatuous, group action was magnificent. A dozen or more heads appeared on the crest of the bank and a wave of clansmen came rushing down towards me. Grasping door handles, mudguards, bumpers and wheel hubs, anything that stood proud of the structure, they hauled and heaved, grunting and sweating in the hot summer evening, until the car was half way up the slope. And they would have restored it to the road had not a passing salmon fisherman offered the winch on his Land Rover to complete the matter.

After I had gratefully stood my hand I set off on the short journey to Meyrick. My first impression that the car was unscathed was false. It was only possible to drive it straight ahead by holding the steering in full left lock and I wondered how I was going to cope with bends.

It was yet another hot day. On the beach a handful of select tourists and visitors were turning salmon-pink under a blazing sun or soaking in luke-warm water in a bay alive with jellyfish while Dobbin and I, running with sweat, were earning our livings in the dark brown forest. From a vantage point at the top of a fire-break I had just seen John Oak's white Jaguar reach the end of the navigable road. He got out and started to climb towards me, accompanied by his two Alsatians.

'I see you're going it alone now, Frere', he remarked as he wiped his face irritably with a handkerchief, 'What happened to Wilson?'

'He had an accident', I replied guardedly.

He turned up his eyes to Heaven. 'Oh, aye. No surprise. Never a safe moment for anyone when you're around. Is he bad?'

'Oh no, he broke two fingers.'

'Dragging, I suppose. Probably too tired to see what he was at.'

'Well, actually we were doing a bit of mountaineering. A stone fell on his hand.'

'Marvellous! Is he likely to recover or have you ruined him for the rest of his working life?'

'He'll be fine. He'll be back within a month or so.'

'That's too late for me. Now look, man, you're neither doing this job nor leaving it alone. This one-man health farm of yours isn't suiting my pocket. If you can do without money I can't, and we happen to be running short of timber at the mill. The puckle sticks you've sent in this month won't pay my time or petrol for coming here and giving you a row. While you're larkin' about here I've a good contractor with a wife, four kids and two horses to feed, and I'm sending him here next week. You can't say I didn't warn you.'

'No. I can't say that', I acknowledged.

'Right', said John Oak, and a more kindly expression formed behind his sweat, 'but I'll not let you down. Do you want to go on working?'

'Most certainly. I have to –'

'Balls to that. It's not the way I see it. But have you ever driven a lorry?'

'Yes, most kinds. In the RAF.'

'That's good. Now I'll tell you what I want you to do –'

John Oak's offer of fresh employment coincided with a change in our domestic plans. Our arrangement to live in Chiefy Wilson's house excluded the months of July, August and the first half of September when he was accustomed to obtain high rents from visitors and we had no other base on the coast. My predilection for a vagrant life-style still fell short of offering my long-suffering wife a bunk in a woodsman's cabin. It was therefore with a feeling of things falling nicely into place, at least from my point of view, that I listened to what he had to propose.

There was a certain amount of cut timber lying in isolated places at the head of forest tracks, beyond the reach of Oak's big diesels. As soon as his new contractor got under way there would be more. To avoid the expense of double handling his plan was to provide me with a four-wheel drive vehicle which could go to the most inaccessible bundles of logs and take them direct to Inverness. He would pay me to load and drive the stuff at so much per ton, to be weighed on arrival. 'Just the kind of strong-man stuff you enjoy, Frere!' he said, having had wind of my former activities in the weight-lifting world, 'since no doubt you'll be doing it all yourself. Don't break my lorry's springs, that's all I ask. They'll only take so much. At the price I'm giving you there'll be a fat pay packet at the end of the week. Good luck, now.' He whistled up his two dogs who piled into the white Jaguar and then he departed briskly in the direction of Inverness.

The plan had its advantages. It was, in fact, the answer to a pressing problem, the question of where we should stay until the autumn. If I could persuade Joan to give up her independence for a few weeks and live beneath my mother's roof all would be well. They had been much better friends since she and Richard had returned from the south. I wanted to believe that this amiable trend would continue and found it easy to do so for I have always had an uncritical belief in the fairy-tale ending.

Joan was not pleased at being withdrawn from the sun and sea and deposited in the gloomy suburban villa where her days consisted in partnering my aging parent in endless games of Canasta and Halma and taking ungracious Domino for short walks on his lead. The dog had a total fixation on his former owners and never lost an opportunity of escaping from my mother's merciless kindness and bounding across the town until he reached their door. There he would howl at the top of his not inconsiderable voice until my mother was notified and sent Joan in a taxi to pick up the prisoner.

My wife, hoping that it would not last forever, suffered all this in praiseworthy silence.

In contrast my own life was full and satisfying. The Bedford Series QL lorry which Oak provided was great sport to drive for its capabilities in the roughest ground were endless. Morning after morning, before the sun was up, I would urge it backwards up rutted tracks and open hillsides until I found a pile of logs. Then I would load it with four or five tons of timber and move cautiously down to the cabin which had been taken from the Kerry and now stood near the main road at Gairloch. With the fine hunger which only violent physical exercise can bring I wolfed a large breakfast, fed Dobbin his grace-and-favour handful of oats – the bulk of his diet, as an idle horse, was supplied by the grass around the cabin – and started on the seventy-mile trip to Inverness and John Oak's mills. My journey there was seldom made without halts for brief swims in the tepid lochs and rivers which lay on my way. In Inverness my timber was weighed and unloaded, I called upon wife and mother for a quick lunch and a few words and then drove back to Gairloch. The return journey did not take long. The lorry, freed of its load rushed along like a sports-car; its high cabin provided a view of the road and its tight blind curves which cars did not have. The QL had a look of authority and its high, square face was daunting: in all the weeks I travelled on that single-track road I do not remember ever having to enter a passing place.

When I came back to Gairloch it was usually early evening and in the first days before the money fever gripped me I contented myself with a climb on An Groban or a ride on Dobbin's back to my favourite river pool. This was a place where the stream warmed its waters on a hundred yards of open slabs before compressing itself into a narrow funnel. Here it dashed down steeply for a good twenty feet and burst in a smother of spray. There was a scoop in the rock, the shape of a man's body, where the spray was strongest and in this scoop I would sit for an hour at a time while Dobbin cropped the grass and the sun went down beyond the headline of Skye. The horse's hooves crushed a heavy scent from the bog myrtle and from a tall grove of rhododendrons a few birds twittered lazily while dragon-flies whizzed and whirred in the quiet air. Any concept of the Garden of Eden must needs vary with the individual but this was mine. It was the epitome of sensuality, the very crown of joyful idleness.

When I was done with it I would put on my bathing trunks and urge Dobbin into a fast trot so that the wind of his motion might dry me. Our way back to the cabin led us past the big hotel. It was stimulating to gallop by and feel the admiration in the eyes of young lady guests sitting outside in their deck chairs drinking gins and tonics.

As the rainless days went on and August brought fresh waves of heat, the River Kerry began to dry up, trapping hundreds of salmon in shallow, rock-locked, pools. Poaching lost its meaning when any number of fish could be removed by their tails by merely reaching down into the water: the fish became a universal staple diet. Our friends at the schoolhouse invited me to dine: there was salmon. I cooked it in my poor fashion and ate huge chunks of it with my potatoes. I compressed it thickly into sandwiches. The forester's wife took pity on my solitary state and sent her husband with a dozen steaks: I shuddered and gave them to the horse. I took two peerless specimens to my mother's house and implored Joan not to cook them until I was on my way. She smiled darkly at my protests and informed me that the glut was universal; even in Inverness they were selling at half the usual price. My mother had already bought a fine fish which was to be served, as a *treat*, for me. I slipped Domino a couple of secret handfuls where he lurked beneath the table. The ungrateful brute was promptly sick. Well, it was either him or me.

On my way back to the coast I was preoccupied with the thought of that king who had died of a surfeit of lampreys. My stomach rolled and heaved and my head swam so that I could hardly keep the lorry on the road. At Gairloch I fell to the ground and vomited from a kneeling position. The waves of nausea followed each other in such quick succession that it was not worth going to bed. By five thirty I was as empty as an unfurnished house and too weak even to crawl to the cabin. I fell forward into the dew and went into a coma. The hot sun woke me a few hours later. I was glad to be alive but displeased to find that Dobbin was nowhere to be seen. A creature of habit, I could not imagine where he had gone and was in no state of health to conduct an immediate search.

The stifling morning did little to improve my condition. I dragged myself up the two steps into the cabin only to find a naked slab of margarine beset by a swarm of bluebottles. It set me back. I went outside and pressed myself a bed in deep bracken where I slept until mid-day. When I woke, weak but no longer nauseous, there was still no sign of Dobbin.

By late afternoon I had scoured the countryside without success. I had enquired about him at the general store, at the police station, at the farm and other places where I had ridden him. I drove the QL to his former haunts at the Kerry Falls and it was on my way back to Gairloch that I had my first news of him. The bus from Achnasheen drew into a passing place and the driver waved me down. He knew Dobbin and me well and now he told me that he had seen the horse feeding near the road for Poolewe, four miles to the north. He suggested that I park the lorry and come with him as he made his evening run in that direction. Then if I found the horse I could ride him back.

In fact he was not where the driver had seen him but three or four miles further north. It was only by chance that I happened to see his head-down silhouette on a distant hillock, small but clear in the afterglow. I stormed feebly up the slope to where he cropped: 'Where the hell have you been?' In answer he gave me an incurious glance and quietly accepted my weight on his back. But my annoyance with him evaporated during the leisurely ride back to Gairloch in the fragrant summer twilight and I wished him goodnight with a mild caution: 'Don't ever do that again, Dobbin. It's not every day that I have the time to look for you.'

It was true that I now had little surplus time. My first wages from this new project were sufficiently exciting to uncover a latent avaricious streak in my nature. Here was a perfect sample of pure piece-work. The amount of money I could earn was directly related to time and effort, and there were twenty-four hours in every day. I had no one to rely on but myself but obversely there was no one to fail me. I have always had an obsession about physical fitness and treat my body as a machine which only reaches perfection when put to a sustained test. Now such a test had come. By loading my lorry at 3 a.m. I found it possible to make two trips to Inverness in a single day. I carried a total of eleven tons of timber over 280 miles and was back in the cabin at 11.30. After three and a half hours' sleep I was just able to get up, although I felt like death. I repeated the previous day's performance. The next morning it was much easier. Like a high-altitude mountaineer I was beginning to acclimatise. By the end of a fortnight I had lost nine pounds in weight and had earned the equivalent, at today's inflated values, of eight hundred and fifty pounds. And it looked as though there was several months' work ahead.

And then Dobbin began to wander in earnest.

I was never sure what made him do it. He had always been 'a horse around the door'. Perhaps he took his redundancy badly: the immense energy stored in his squat frame needed an outlet. Or maybe his feelings were hurt because he had ceased to be the king-pin of the operation as he had been for so long.

From time to time I grudgingly allowed myself a day off. Dobbin's second disappearance coincided with one of them. I woke early from habit, though later than usual and gave a glance at his usual patch of grass. It was empty. I swore silently and shouted to him through the door. There was a chance that he was no further away than a fringe of trees around the clearing so without immediate anxiety I put on my kettle for tea. As I lit the primus stove there was a bang on the door which I had closed against the early morning midges. It sounded like the horse's customary greeting. I gave him a few moments to reflect on his crimes then shouted: 'You'll get no bread from me this morning, you wandering bugger!' There was a short silence, then what seemed like a grunt, then a further bang. I grinned, opened wide the door and tossed out a stale half loaf. It hit the local policeman, Sergeant McKern, full in the face.

'Oh, my God', I said, 'I'm sorry!' I added lamely, 'I thought it was the horse', but the Sergeant seemed less put out by my assault than the train of thought initiated by my false surmise. 'That horse, is it?' he demanded, brushing bread crumbs from his hair, 'Where is the devil now? That is what I am wanting to know.'

My relationship with the Sergeant had already been soured by my failure to license the Fraser Nash and I was unhappy to cross swords with him again. I said defensively: 'He's not far away, he doesn't wander much.'

'You tell me that! Most often you are not here to see. He is up and down the road, blocking traffic. Last night a woman from America came to the station asking for the

sheriff. Your horse – oh yes, it was yours: there is none like it
– was standing in the middle of the road up at the Kerry and
wouldn't let her pass. When she blew her horn and pressed
against its legs it . . .'

'Don't say it', I groaned, envisaging damages, 'it kicked
in her radiator, I suppose.'

'Fortunately not, but it committed a nuisance. It shit
upon her bonnet. She used that very word', said McKern
disapprovingly.

'Some Americans do. Plain folk', I observed.

'Ach no, she was a great lady, just. We got to talking
when I had written down her complaint. Her worry was for
the horse, you understand? It would seem that her name is
Mackenzie and her husband is the owner of a great store in
America. Or rather, he was – he is now dead, she said, of the
overwork. She came here, looking for his ancestors, for it
would seem that one, Shamus Mackenzie was sent away on
a ship by the wicked laird of that day. Aye, 'twas the time of
the Clearances.'

'Best thing that ever happened to him', I remarked inad-
visedly.

'So it might be said', agreed McKern to my surprise. 'It
is surely a great country for the promotion. I shall forget the
matter of the horse if I have your promise to tie it tightly in
your absences. Tonight, especially, I would not wish for the
disturbance. Mrs Mackenzie has been so kind as to bid me
to the hotel for drinks and the talk.'

I promised him, he left and I went in search of Dobbin.

I did not find him but he returned late that night and I
tethered him to a stake with a new climbing rope. He
chewed through it. I tried a light chain used for securing
timber. He pulled out the stake. I asked a Kerrysdale
farmer if I might use his sheep fank. Dobbin demolished a
dry stone dyke and fifteen feet of fence in two consecutive
nights. Nothing could keep him in. My work routine was
broken and when I went to Inverness it was with a dread of
what I might find on my return. Sometimes he would come
back of his own accord, more often I had to search the

countryside for clues as to where he was. He had given up his road patrol and had taken to grazing harmlessly in the high grass around the rocky roots of An Groban. But there was no guarantee that this was a permanent change of habit.

I was growing totally exhausted. Constant worry is more wearying than the hardest physical work. My nights at Gairloch were regularly interrupted and I dared not stay overnight in Inverness. A rational person would have found a simple solution by selling the horse but I was fond of Dobbin and had a stubborn wish to keep him. Then one late evening I brought my empty lorry to a halt outside the cabin and saw McKern where Dobbin should have been. I knew by his expression as he fingered a short length of broken chain that my hand was about to be forced.

He began, with preamble: 'I think the devil himself must be in it. This time it is a *complaint* and it is myself that is making it. Yon brown fiend has eaten my winter cabbages, stood on my bairn's foot and frighted my wife to near her grave. It is impounded in my garage where it will remain at your own expense until I have your word that you will send it away.'

I had the bleakest imaginings of what Dobbin might do when captive in a strange garage and hastily agreed to deportation after extradition. 'Well, then', said McKern, 'come down to the Strath with me and let me be rid of it quick. I do not care to leave my wife and bairn in such company.'

McKern's garage was a light structure of wood frame and asbestos sheet. The doors were secured by a leaning tree trunk but I was alarmed to see a half opened window in its side. A single glance at the policeman's cabbage patch was enough to show me that his lovingly tended crop had been entirely uprooted.

There was a shuffling noise from inside the building, then an angry neigh. That unrepentant sound coupled with the animal's vandalism infuriated me. I shouted: 'Keep still, Dobbin, you bloody brute.' I should have kept quiet but I had reached breaking point. So had McKern's garage.

Dobbin's head came through the window. For a fatal moment I failed to see what he intended. When I shouted and made a run for his head it was too late. The pressure of the frame on his neck was all the stimulous he needed; he hadn't worked for ages, now he'd show what a bully horse he was, as he had done at Moy so long ago. His shoulders heaved, there was a sharp crack, asbestos splintered like glass and he came forward with the window frame round his neck. Behind him part of the garage roof collapsed.

He looked at us. There was triumph in his yellow eyes. Then he lowered his head, the window frame came free and landed at McKern's feet with a crash.

That night I punished him for the first and last time. I gave him no food. I was beside myself with annoyance, exhaustion and indecision. McKern, considering the extent of his loss, had shown great restraint though when I had left him he had still been in a state of some shock. I think that relief at my avowed intention to rid his parish of my horse had overcome all other emotions. Now I hobbled Dobbin's back legs, knocked a link into the chain, drove the stake yet further into the ground and connected another rope to the cabin door. I was hardly able to keep my eyes open when I flopped onto my straw mattress but before I went to sleep I had decided what must be done. There was a horse box in Gairloch which might be hired: Dobbin would go to Inverness in it where I would sell him to one of Oak's contractors. He would only be happy working and most of the contractors I had come across were kind to the beasts on which they relied.

I passed that night in the kind of sleep that makes death seem like an uneasy nap. I ceased to exist between ten o'clock at night and the same hour in the morning, when I woke with a great start to a rush of uneasy thoughts and fears which were justified by a single glance. Dobbin had gone, taking the stake with him.

My first thought was that he would have gone back to the scene of his latest crime. But he was not there. From a concealed point of vantage I saw with regret that the rest of McKern's ruptured garage had collapsed, but nothing to suggest that the horse had returned. I went round the village and walked a few miles along the main road to the north, examined the strip of grass below An Groban and crossed into the Kerry Valley. Here I found hoof marks in the dust and some fresh dung. I knew then where he would be.

I found him at five o'clock exactly, standing in the place where the cabin had once been, on the edge of the bank, opposite the long spires of the silver spruce. He looked up when I came and there was a questioning expression on his face as if to say: 'This is where I used to be fed, and it's my time. Give me my oats and hay and let's forget the trouble I've been to you. I'll be a good horse from now on, I promise.'

But I knew he couldn't keep his promise because the devil finds work for idle hooves. My mind was vacant of ideas but I cut him free of the stake which he had dragged behind him and then mounted his broad back. As we ambled down the road which was so familiar to us both I became a prey to growing nostalgia. There was a touch of autumn in the cooling evening air; its slight chill had clear varnished the dusty colours and it was very quiet in the glen. I noticed that the long summer had dried up all the water in the river. The hydro pipe still sang but the falls were a flight of peat-stained steps. I wondered how my pearl farmers were making out. Then I heard an odd echo, the double beat of horses' hooves sounding from behind us. 'Wo, Dobbin' I said. A cavalcade was coming towards us: it consisted of two grey horses, small but well-rounded, two men, a woman and a youth. One of the horses was drawing a light cart. The other, smaller than its companion, was festooned with an array of pots and pans which made a cheerful tinkle as it walked. The humans were dark with wood smoke and gypsy ancestry: I waited for them to overtake us to see if they looked kind.

' 'Tis a grand evening, is't not?' remarked the man in a

thick Irish voice. They say the Irish are good to horses. 'Fine indeed', I answered him, 'and has been a wonderful summer.' I gave Dobbin a prod; he moved away, eyeing the other horses with his customary speculation.

We rode in silence for a while, then the man said: 'Sartin 'tis an impertinence to ask but were you t'inking o' sellin' your harse? 'Tis a fine creature. Is't used to the shafts?'

'No, to the wood.'

' 'Twould larn the shafts, gi'en patience.' He hesitated then repeated: 'Would you be wishin' to sell him, Sarr?'

'To good company I would sell him.'

He gave me a look of respect. 'Ye can see me own harses. 'Tis age and nothing else that ails 'em. And yet me wife's more like to be put to the knackers than t' harses!' He grinned darkly into the sunset and the woman nodded without offence. 'How much would ye be askin' for the harse?'

'Forty pieces of silver.'

'Eh, wot would that be then, Sarr?'

I murmured to myself: 'The going rate in treachery, I suppose', then added aloud, 'I'm sorry, I was joking. Five pounds to you for a quick sale.'

'Done, Sarr,' said the Irishman, surprised, 'and what would ye tak' for the collar?'

'Nothing', I said, 'you can have the collar.' After Dobbin I would never want another horse.

He looked at me in wonder. I began to dismount. 'Will ye not ride wi' us to the Gairloch?' he asked.

'No', I said, as I took from him a crumpled, greasy note. 'I'll go on foot through the wood. There's a path which leads to my house. Goodbye, Dobbin, do behave yourself.' I turned to his new owner. 'Yes, that's his name – Dobbin. Treat him well and he'll repay your kindness!'

I ran up the bank, not daring to look back. Then I paused in the cool, friendly wood. From the road the sound of horses' hooves merged and echoed in the still air before fading into silence behind the long avenue of trees.

Dobbin, even in his most perverse moments, had been a good companion and I missed him badly. Even before I reached the cabin I began to regret my hasty expedience and more than once in a night of broken sleep I had to resist an urge to seek out the gypsies and buy him back at any price. In the small hours a puff of wind nudged the open cabin door and my heart warmed to the sound: 'Oh, you're back, are you', I cried but there was no dark shape against the background of misty trees. For once in my life I felt a sense of loneliness. As soon as dawn had come I got up and put away his bag of oats and drinking pail which had acquired the potent poignancy of a lost child's toys.

A combination of events brought Joan back to Gairloch in early October. Richard, who had been with her at my mother's house, had started preparatory schooling in St Andrews at the autumn term. Shortly after this my own routine changed: I no longer made my daily trips to Inverness. By mid September the tapestry of summer had been showing marked signs of wear and a few heavy showers of rain easily convinced me that my days of driving timber down the peaty forest tracks were numbered. Soon they would be quagmires from which even the resourceful QL would find it hard to escape with more than the smallest load. The answer was to concentrate on the awkward places while access was still possible and assemble all the remaining timber in a flat field adjacent to the main road. Thereafter I should be independent of the weather. This local haulage might take about three weeks and since Meyrick would be available in November, it seemed a good idea for Joan to join me at once. The short-term accommodation problem was solved when much to my surprise she suggested sharing my cabin. It was not a thing I would have asked of her. Perhaps the strain of looking after my demanding mother had made the decision the lesser of two evils. At any rate she came and after a single shocked glance and the just remark that I was a slatternly creature only fit to inhabit a cave she worked her own brand of domestic miracle. The wooden hut became a wholesome, if essentially temporary, dwelling. One evening as we sat by the red hot woodsman stove eating fillet steak and mushrooms on tin plates she remarked: 'Do you know I'm quite enjoying this?' I nodded with some satisfaction. I certainly was. It was the kind of undemanding life-style that suited me down to the ground. I could hardly remember what the cabin had looked like before she came. I had burnt the bunks and bedding in the stove and we had brought a small bed from Inverness which now occupied a corner of the shack. It was made up with fresh white sheets and my pyjamas shared a space with her nightdress. I remembered with shame how I had worn the same shirt day and night for a week. Reaching out to a small cupboard whose rough boards had been bleached white and lined with greaseproof paper, I withdrew a whisky bottle and two glasses emblazoned with the family crest: 'Like a drink?' I suggested.

'We'll have it later, as a toddy. How about some tea?'

'Why not? Oh, damn, there's no water. I'll go down to the burn.'

'No I will. It's a wonderful warm wet night. I love the rain, as you know. Give me the torch.'

'Are you sure? It's raining cats and dogs.'

But she went and I sat and reflected on the joys of domesticity. A few more minutes went by than were strictly necessary, it was only twenty yards to the bridge, an old estate one, which crossed a small narrow gorge. From the other side you scrambled down to the stream; we called it the water hole. After another thirty quickening heartbeats I decided I had better give her a hand. I opened the cabin door; the rain sluiced against my face like a big wet kiss. It was dark but not so dark as to make the outline of the bridge invisible. There was no one on it, nor walking the track between it and the cabin. As I ran through the streaming gloom I felt a quick sense of panic, a fear of human dis-appearance which has always been one of my personal phobias and was then still raw after Richard's performance at Badachro. It is part of the ransom one pays in return for a family. I had just time to shout a nervous joke: 'Where have you got to this time, Captain Oates?' when I saw that the planks in the centre of the bridge were missing.

Joan lay half in and half out of the water beside a large boulder. She was moaning slightly and one of her legs was extended stiffly. It was not easy to restore her to the track without inflicting additional pain and it was twenty minutes before we were back in the cabin. My worst fear had been that the twelve-foot fall into the rocky stream bed might have damaged her back but this at least was ground-less. But the facts were bad enough. She had gone straight down, as though through an executioner's trap, and her bent left knee had struck the edge of a rock, splitting the patella cleanly across. She didn't say much in her shock but it was plain that she was in great pain. I remember thinking dazedly as I drove the QL to the doctor's house in Gairloch that here was deliberate confusion on the part of the Fates who apportion human destiny. She had received a moun-taineer's injury; through no fault of her own she had been exposed to the chance of broken bones. She had been put casually in risk in a sphere of activity that was not hers. So, to a lesser degree, had Bob. 'Never a safe moment when you're around', Oak had said and the joke had been proved harsh and true. But this time at least the Fates were exon-erated from all blame for in my careless fashion I had forgotten to tell her that the planks in the bridge were rotten.

Dr Macrae was a small nervous man who saw medicine as a calling rather than a profession. He was used to being called to places which would have struck dismay into the hearts of his medical contemporaries in comfortable town practices, and the range of his ministrations was unres-tricted. The removal of a human tooth or the sewing up of an animal belly were taken in his stride and the journey right up to the cabin door in the bucking, slithering lorry was to him just another visit. He examined my damaged wife with a cool, confident kindness, gave her a shot of morphia and remarked: 'There's no injury beyond the knee-cap. We can't get her out tonight but I'll have an ambulance drive as near as possible in the morning. I'd not bother you to drive me back to my house – it's not far over the hill – but there's a wifey in the Strath a week over her time with her first and the bairn'll not come easy.'

In the morning an ambulance edged up into the wood and Joan was taken to it on a stretcher. The small stream was now a torrent and a gusting wind shook water from the trees like dogs fresh from a swim. I sat beside her as she lay tight lipped in the narrow ambulance bunk. Our destination was a hospital in Inverness.

She had an operation and many weeks of pain. The patella knitted but a web of adhesions strangled the joint. Each day the movement of her leg had to be forcibly extended, inch by painful inch. It was to be years before full flexion was restored to the limb.

I left her in hospital and went back to work. I was like an automaton, shocked and disconsolate. My sleep was broken by anxious dreams. The rain never ceased and the wood was engulfed in a perpetual mist. The QL had met its match; it constantly bogged down in a battlefield of its own making. The logs that remained were scattered and remote; it was often easier to manhandle them to the lorry rather than risk driving the lorry to them. I was soaked to the skin from morning to evening and covered in yellow mud. My spirits had reached a low point. Thus deflated I had no wish to see any of the people in Gairloch who had become our friends and spent my last days there in dogged work and bitter self-accusation, a solitary hermit, unwashed and unshaven, in his little wooden hut. Then one day, almost to my surprise, I searched the dripping wood for log piles and found none: I loaded my lorry with everything it could carry and came back to Inverness. By the end of another month I had driven all the timber into Oak's mill and began to wonder what fresh work he had in mind for me.

'There's not much', he said, 'since you're still on your own and any fool could see you don't give a tinker's cuss about going into business seriously. You disappoint me, Frere!' and added his oft repeated jibe: 'I thought you'd have bought me out by now but I can see that the whole thing's a great big joke to you. Give my best respects to your good lady. By the way, I was sorry to hear what you've done to her. No, don't say it', he went on as he saw I was about to bum about my recent huge earnings, 'that was just a flash in the pan. You've a tough body and enough energy to drive a train; I know that they call you Fresh Air Frere, but it'll get you nowhere unless you learn to organise men. You've made a bit, right enough, and if you could get that kind of work and do it for thirty years you could call the Prime Minister a poor relation, but you'd kill yourself in no time. And in any case', he added primly, 'that kind of thing's not for the likes of you.'

'I wish I knew what was. I'm not qualified for any profession.'

'Balls!' he said rudely, 'and don't go blaming your parents now. That's an easy way out. Ever thought of using your brains? You've written a book, haven't you?'

I admitted it. 'Well, write another. But it's plain you won't take my advice. Well, just to sicken you I'll offer you one last job.'

'What's that?'

'Cutting up pit props in the railway yard near my mill. There's no glamour about it and your friends in town can see how far you've fallen. Aren't *both* your kids at boarding school now? Well they're going to love this. Children talk, you know.'

I saw his point although it seemed faintly hypocritical. He meant that if you wished to soil your hands with manual labour it should be done in private. What would pass as an eccentricity in the hidden woods might be construed as degeneracy in a town where my family had been held in respect. I had to acknowledge that I didn't relish the idea of working in a rail siding. But I didn't want to give in while there was still money to be made and while Joan remained in hospital it was good to be on hand. I decided to make a final all-out effort in the timber trade and when she was better we would return to the Bungalow, put a roof on it as planned and seek some more acceptable occupation.

When I broke the news to her, Joan was firm. Feeling bitter about her stiff leg and tired of my vagrancy, she was in no mood to fit in with my cut-price, easy way out plans. 'Work there', she said, 'and I'll leave you. I know how your mind works. As soon as I'm out of here it'll be back to your mother's house and you'll go on fooling about in that slum. And I don't want the Bungalow either. No as soon as I can travel I'm going south to my own people and I won't come back until you've settled yourself and found a decent place for me to live.'

From this ultimatum she would not be moved. Even my mother, delighted as she was with the prospect of cosseting me made sarcastic remarks about my job. Such total opposition made me all the more stubborn. I accepted Oak's proposal and on the day Joan left for Sussex I started cutting pit props in Shipland's Yard.

It wasn't a pleasant place. On the fringe of the town's new industrial site, it was a rough triangle of hard-packed earth and sawdust furnished with a few broken-down sheds and soiled by dog turds, beer cans and a great variety of litter. It was flanked by a bakery, a railway bridge and a bus station and even after these many years I am moved to a reluctant nostalgia by the merged smells of baking and diesel oil, though their chance combination is rare. Many people passed through the yard on their ways to and from work but it only had two residents, both of whom lived in sheds. One was a tipsy and aged tinker known as Twenty Pockets from his habit of wearing several overcoats simultaneously; the other was a young man with a well worn face called Ian Macbeth.

The making of wooden pit props from forest thinnings was simple enough but it needed two men. Using a small circular saw, the sawyer held the thick end of the tree and cut it to a length appropriate to its girth while his assistant supported the small end. John Oak had made it plain that if I indulged my passion for gadgets and one-manship by constructing a device which would eliminate a helper, he would get rid of me. Thus my first act in the yard was to look about for an employee.

Ian Macbeth was an obvious first choice. He was 'living in', so to speak, and appeared to have no regular job. As ill-favoured as Caliban, as simple as Barnaby Rudge, he was an amenable, hard-working chap with a shrewd and practical twist to him and a single weakness: in drink he was riotous and his violence had a specific object. It was generally believed that as a child he had been boarded out in the house of a female Fagin, an old woman of criminal habits and maniac temper, who set him illicit tasks and beat him black and blue when he failed to perform them. A hatred and fear of all old women had formed in his punch-drunk mind. When he was sober, which was most of the time, he was able to contain his devil but give him a few drinks and no female over sixty-five, or who looked that age, was safe from violent assault. He called them 'pigs o' hell' or 'Oaps', pronounced as spelt, from the letters which defined their status.

He agreed at once to work for me for a very low wage. I had been warned not to give him too much money for his needs were small and any surplus cash would encourage him to break out.

We settled down to a steady routine. Every morning a load of thinnings was dumped in the yard and by nightfall it would be cut up and graded as props of various sizes. The Coal Board was now requiring pit props to be peeled, stripped cleanly of their bark, and this meant an extra man. I thought of Twenty Pockets, who had once been in trade, and invited him to attend to this monotonous and un-demanding task. To my surprise the old tramp jumped at the idea and set to with a will. Unlike my other helper he worked well on alcohol and could neatly de-bark a hundred trees or more on what I took to be dilute methylated spirits.

The time soon came when we found we could handle two loads a day. I felt it was time the men had a bonus. I gave them five pounds each. Twenty Pockets slipped his note into the depths of his third overcoat while Ian said: 'Keep it for me, Boss' but forgetting how I had been warned I told him he had earned it.

The next morning there was no sign of him. His shed was empty and he was nowhere in the yard. I went over to Twenty Pockets' bunk at the far end of an old engine shed. The old tramp was snoring heavily behind his matted rug of beard. I gave him a prod: 'Morning, Pockets. It's time to get going. By God, it's cold in here. Can't you block out the wind?'

'Aye, Frar.' He never managed my name in recognisable form. 'It's like the arsehole o' the world, but I got me coats. Hav'na had 'em off me back in thirty year or more, man an' boy. Give us a fag.' I gave him one and lit it. 'Did you see Ian last night?' I enquired. 'I can't find him around this morning.' Pockets inhaled suicidally and gave a knowing look. 'I'm no' surprised at that. You give him money and he got drink. I reckon he's oot hunting the auld bags. He'll be hidin' doon Shipland Lane, waiting to bash one or two of 'em. Better go after him Frar, 'fore he gets the jail.'

I hastily departed and after a short wait was rewarded by the sight of Ian Macbeth, dirty, dejected but with a crusading light in his eye, lurking in the doorway of an empty house. He had a short pit prop in his hand. Not far away, and advancing steadily, was a small group of senior female citizens. I ran up to Ian and tried to wrest the weapon away from him but he resisted me strongly. One look at his mangled face told me that at this moment he was very mad indeed. His bloodshot eyes rolled, his mouth was open and his tongue twitched like a dying soldier behind the broken battlements of his teeth. Finally I dragged the prop from his hands and tried to turn him away from the objects of his fury but he broke from me and danced like a dervish in front of the women. 'Hags, bags, Oaps', he chanted, 'hags, bags,

Oaps. Ye'd kill me would ye no, but I'll no let ye! Kick in me face would ye? Hellish old bags, pigs o'hell!'

The pensioners had broken formation and were in full flight, fat backsides rolling obscenely in their sudden alarm. I dragged the screaming Ian by his coat in the general direction of the mill. Overhead windows opened and becurlered heads appeared. I wondered uneasily what Joan would have thought of it.

Yet when he wasn't berserk Ian was as rational as the next man and he had that special kind of practical mind that is sometimes found in simple people. It was soon evinced in his attitude to the waste wood from the pit prop cutting which traditionally becomes the sawmiller's property. Ian saw a possibility for profit in it. Lying in the yard was a big, old-fashioned cart, between whose shafts many a railway horse had grown tired. One afternoon I found that my assistant had loaded it with firewood blocks which he had previously cut on our saw. 'We'll take it around the houses, Boss', he announced in answer to my question, 'after five o'clock, and mak' a pile o' money oot o' it.' I was amused though slightly alarmed. 'If you like. But mind you bring me the money. We don't want any more Oap hunts.' I was pleased to indulge him. Later he left the yard, his thick-set body bent in the shafts of the cart which must have carried nearly half a ton of logs. I didn't know how late he worked that night but when I met him in the morning he dutifully offered me a canvas bag filled to the brim with florins.

His round soon grew. In the first few days he made twice his week's wages and then asked me to spare him in the early afternoon so that he could do two deliveries. He was emphatically honest and the customers whom he had taken from under the nose of an established firewood merchant, unable to compete with our no-overhead bargain prices, loved him. His gnome-like figure and goggling, cheerful face made him welcome wheresoever wood was burnt. In that cold winter that meant almost every house. Only once did I hear, and then from his own lips, how he had discriminated against those whom he held in such subconscious hatred. He had put a bag into the wood shed of a surly octogenarian who remarked: 'I wonder your boss don't put down the price a bit for us old folks – give us a special rate, like. Two bob'll ruin us.'

'You an Oap, then?' asked Ian, knowing full well she must be.

'Eh, what's that?' enquired the crone.

'An Old Age Pensioner', repeated Ian, carefully.

'Aye', said the bargainer, hopefully.

'Aye', echoed Ian, 'he will that. It'll be half a crown to you.' And he got it. 'Auld bitches', he told me later. 'You know, Boss, they got more money than you and me put together.'

In order to keep our customers happy we had to cut more pit props. Ian's increasing involvement in our new line tended to upset the balance of production and I decided that I ought to employ another man. No sooner had I let it be known that I was looking for a full-time help than my first applicant stood before me in the sawdust. He had been hanging around the yard for days looking for a start. His name was Raymond Webster, a sturdy self-confident youth of seventeen. He agreed to the small wage I offered but implied that if he gave me satisfaction he would look for something better later on. I liked his attitude which showed he held himself in some esteem

Ian and Raymond, the one complacent, the other ambitious, had this in common: both wanted me to set up as a firewood merchant on my own account. No one could doubt big returns in the short term but I had been in such a situation before. From Oak I was getting a weekly income though it did not compare with that from the previous haulage venture. But it was certain. Firewood was selling well, it was winter and coal was expensive; but who would want our produce in warm summer days? 'We would stock up in the summer', urged Raymond, wise beyond his years, 'buy a birch wood and work it. You'd have a good going business in no time at all.' I demurred: the spectre of too hasty expansion had familiar eye sockets in a naked skull.

But the boys were adamant and importunate; in their deferential way they had ganged up on me and were pushing me in a direction which disturbed my new-found prudence. I agreed to think about it in order to keep them quiet.

The cart was becoming very decrepit. It was being loaded with enormous weights for Raymond had joined Ian on the evening round and they piled a mountain of logs upon it. While one pulled the other pushed and the ancient vehicle sagged and creaked. Then the inevitable happened and one of the wheels collapsed; the thing fell over on its side in the street. The boys came back to me with determined looks.

'The cart's dead, Boss', grinned Ian, waiting for Raymond to fire the next shot.

'I think I know where we can borrow another', I said, after having heard the details. Raymond Webster was resolute: 'No need, Boss. The cart was too small anyway and', here he lowered his voice, 'Ian thinks the Oaps are laughing at him. He'll no' push a cart again. I've told the customers we'll be round in a lorry next week.'

'You'll be round in a *what*?'

'A lorry. I know where we can get one, a Ford Thames with a twelve-foot platform. Just the job, and only sixty quid. Come on, Boss, you can't let us down.'

I saw that I couldn't, and my pulse quickened at the thought of new machinery. Once again I cast caution to the winds: 'You win. We're going into business but don't ever say it was my idea. You'll probably be out of a job within weeks, both of you. Where is this lorry? Let's go and buy the damn thing.'

The Ford Thames which Raymond had heard about was stubby and solid. It could carry sixty bags of wood on its platform. Though its powerful V8 engine had a raging thirst, petrol was less than five shillings a gallon in those glorious far-off days.

There was only one immediate drawback. Neither of my boys had driving licences and I had some reservations against exposing myself to the general public in my new role. I had brooded upon Joan's attitude to social denigration and was convinced that once she knew I was hawking firewood around the houses she would never come back. In Shipland's Yard I had remained unseen. Not wishing to confuse Ian or Raymond on the finer points of social brinkmanship I firmly stated that I wished to remain a mystery and if I were to drive the lorry it must be late in the evening and in disguise. This fitted in with the work pattern as we cut props and firewood by day and started our round at 6 p.m. Ian and Raymond rode on the platform amid the bags while I sat at the wheel, never leaving the cab, concealed behind a balaclava helmet and a pair of sunglasses. Sometimes curious urchins would climb on to the step of the vehicle to get a glimpse of the man of mystery who neither turned his head nor opened his mouth but the boys scared them away and my anonymity remained intact. To inquisitive customers I was 'the Driver' or for less obvious reasons 'the Farmer' and I let the boys spread the legend that I had once been burned in an accident and was shy of showing my face. One frosty night in early March Ian and Raymond were offered drams by an hospitable buyer who added a kind afterthought to her invitation: 'We can't let the Farmer sit out there. Will you not ask him in for a drop o' the creatur?'

'Oh he'd not thank you for the drink', said well instructed Raymond.

'But surely he'll take a cup of tea then?'

'He canna stomach the tea.'

'The poor man. Well at least he'll come in for a warm this cold night?' Raymond was flummoxed but Ian came to his rescue. 'He's fair set on the cold. Ye ken, after his accident. He canny stand to look into the hairt o' a fire.' Ian's dull mind still had a few sharp edges. In the meantime the poor man sat in the steel box of his cab shivering from cold and inactivity and wondering if the time had not come to modify an image that brought him such discomfort.

It was Spring but the weather remained chilly and wet. A

blustering lamb's storm promoted the sale of our goods. And then we suffered our first misfortune in the new series.

Raymond said to me one morning: 'I reckon Ian's going to take a turn, Boss. His head's fair splitting most of the time – you know, where the auld wife cracked him.' It was true that there was an indentation on Ian's skull, said to have been made by a poker. 'Can we get him to see a doctor, do you think?' I enquired. Raymond shook his head: 'No, he's fairt of doctors. He says they'll put him away. An' I think they might. He talks fair queer at times. Only last week he found Twenty Pockets lying pissed out on the sawdust and he said to me: "Oh Cripes, God's dead." And you remember that rowan wood we put out of the way?'

'Yes, it was next to the railway wagons.'

'Well, Ian's been cutting it up with the buck saw. And hiding it.'

'That was a strange thing to do, certainly.'

We had recently been buying in odd loads of wood to help our stocks. People brought it to us in trailers. One bundle had consisted mostly of rowan which burns with a bitter smell and is not liked by the superstitious. To burn the tree which is a sure protection against witches is to invite their malignant attentions. In order to guard against offence I had instructed that it should be put aside. I assumed that for some secret reason Ian was burning it in his bothy stove.

The crisis came a few days later. I had just arrived at the yard when Raymond dashed up to me: 'You'd better come, Boss. Ian'll no' leave his shed, and he's gibbering like a monkey.'

'Has he had drink?'

'I canny smell it. This is no' the drink. He's just stone mad.'

I opened the bothy door. A frying pan, complete with fat, just missed my head: it was accompanied by a half human roar. When he saw that it was me and not the savage virago who had so long tormented his memory he grew quiet, the snarl left his face and was replaced by an expression of cheerful cunning. 'I've something to tell you, Boss', he said through twisted lips.

'What, Ian? Take it easy, old chap.'

'I've done for some of them pigs o' hell. Gave the witches a hand, like.'

Oh lord, I thought, he's been out murdering pensioners. I took him by his shaking shoulders. 'Tell me truthfully about it, Ian. Have you been attacking old ladies?'

'No, no, Boss. Do you take me for a fool? I didn'a want to get mesel hung up. It was so easy, so easy.' He began to croon. 'Put a block in a bag, put a block in a bag, and shove it in a woodshed.' I felt a wave of relief although it was all too sadly clear that Ian's condition was no longer transitory and that here was a job for the professionals. 'I see, Ian. You added some rowan to the birch blocks we sold to our customers. Well that won't do them any harm, will it?'

I shan't forget the look he gave me. It contained a flash of most unholy knowledge. And then he went into peals of maniac laughter. He was still laughing when white-coated attendants took him away in an ambulance to the great hospital on the hill. We did not see him again. But his story had an epilogue for the same evening, as we were preparing for our round, Raymond said to me: 'You're not going to believe this, Boss.'

Nor are you, my readers, but it is true, just the same. At Raymond's request I went with him down the road which we jokingly called 'Oap Avenue' because of the many old women who lived there. 'You see,' said my assistant soberly, 'numbers 7, 12, and 23. Gives you a queer feeling, don't it Boss?'

It did. A very queer feeling. In each house he pointed out the blinds were shut tightly against the light of day. Three pensions would not be drawn that week. The witches, given their chance, had not wasted a minute.

Deprived of Ian the two of us could no longer handle both the firewood and the pit props and my final decision to concentrate on the former coincided with Oak's intention to close down the yard. He had recently changed his policy and proposed to have propping done in the woods. We parted on good terms, neither having let the other down. 'Keep in touch, Frere', he said, 'you're a hell of a man, but good luck to you. I never thought you'd stick it this long. Take my advice, build up steadily and don't try to go it alone. You'll get nowhere that way.'

For a very small sum I bought fifty acres of standing birch near the village of Croy, about ten miles east of Inverness. It was wonderful to be out of the yard and working again in the natural places. In a way I hated to cut down those lovely little trees with their fragrance after rain and the silver varnished bark which is one of Nature's works of art but it is a transitory harvesting. Birch is a wooden weed and will spring up indomitably even when man, the only truly irresponsible species, has burnt the surface of his fair planet to cinders.

I gave up my anonymity. The 'farmer' had become the man with the grey lorry and the big bags of firewood. I believe that a man who dares to do business on his own account has an honourable status no matter what the business is; and after all an honest job is nothing to be ashamed about. I might not have the wit and I certainly lacked the inclination to make my millions in the dusty confines of some city office but to me there was a greater value in the swing of the axe in green woods, the feel of strong muscles and the words, heard at the end of the day, 'These were good logs we had from you last week.'

Now it seemed an amusing idea to give our small business a name. I thought about it but it was Raymond who came up with a title. When we first came to Croy we had to tell our customers we wouldn't be making any deliveries until we had built up stocks. Raymond gave them the message. 'I told them they had better not burn anybody else's sticks until we came round again', he said.

'That's it, Raymond.'

'What, Boss?'

'Our name. Betterburn Firewood Products. I'll stencil it on the lorry tonight. What colour should the letters be do you think? Red or green?'

15 ❧ Calm Sea, Prosperous Voyage and Shipwreck

At the rate of an acre a week it took us nearly a year to cut down the birch wood at Croy. To help us in what was a considerable task we hired part-time labour, a squad of bus drivers and their mates whom we had latterly employed on casual terms at Shipland's Yard. These were sturdy fellows, anxious both to make extra money and to give free vent to their energies, for bus driving is a dangerously sedentary occupation. As shift workers in their own profession each man could only give us four or five hours three days a week but the shifts overlapped and we were never without a strong support force. They were all friends who entered into cheerful competition with each other and the throaty, ironic Inverness humour of these natural comedians gave each day's activities a background of cabaret.

The birch wood grew on flat ground. Most of it was hard and here the trees were smallish, rough-barked and dry, but where there were moist places the birch grew stout and tall, like tent poles holding high a green awning. In winter they sighed and shivered in a north east wind to which the ground was particularly exposed. When it blows from that quarter there is a faint smell of brine and seaweed from the Moray Firth and when you face that way the Monadhliath mountains roll away behind you, their long inclines of heather, scarp and moss-fringed bog rising gently to emphatic cairns. Carr Bridge lies across those hills, beyond twenty miles of open moor and the deep, beautiful valley of the Findhorn and often while I worked or rested I would think about our life there and wonder about our little house. We had never been back although we had passed the entrance to the Station Road a dozen times as we collected our children or returned them to school. It was odd, this inhibition which we felt about it: as though confrontation with that place of wasted years might infect the more contented and progressive present. Also at the back of our minds was a sad concern about what five winters might have done to the house, a fear that was better left unconfirmed.

We lived now in a flat offered to us by a friend in a Victorian house on the outskirts of Inverness. Joan had rejoined me about a month after Betterburn's christening. My repeated assurance that the drab days were over had been a trifle premature but she was not displeased with our new situation. Though as temporary as ever it was as big as I wanted, the income was regular and assured. I had indulged my passion for machinery by buying from John Oak a Canadian Ford four-wheel-drive lorry whose function was to carry out trees from the centre of our roadless wood. Its enormous power and its tank-like ability to grind its way over the most unsurmountable obstacles gave me endless pleasure. But even though we were served by these human and mechanical aids Raymond and I worked immoderate hours, often starting in the wood before the sun was up. By nine at night, our round finished, we were glad to get the weight off our shoulders. It was a six-day week filled with sixty or seventy sweating hours: on the seventh day, like God, we rested and I am sure with equal satisfaction. In the evenings Joan would complain that I was poor company for I often went to sleep in front of the fire, but I was extraordinarily fit and that to me is one of the main justifications for being alive.

In due course we cut our last tree at Croy and moved nearer home. I had heard of a gentleman who owned a rough and rugged woodland of hardwoods on the red scree slopes above Loch Ness. It was only a few miles from Dunain Park, the house where we now lived. Colonel Carson was a gracious lowland Scot who had bravely forsaken the army for a more perilous civilian occupation, that of proprietor of a small crofting estate. Accustomed to being obeyed without the need for tedious explanations and getting things done smartly by the military book, he was genuinely surprised by the resentment which his autocracy aroused in his tenants. He was unaware that the Highlander will be neither hustled nor bossed about without consultation and this ignorance was costing him dear. No sooner did he serve notice to quit upon some troublesome incumbent than he received by return a ruinous and indisputable bill in respect of compensation for generations of improvement upon the property. When I met him he was drowning in litigation: what had begun as an irritation was fast becoming an obsession, and he spoke darkly and only half humorously of firing squads as the speedy answer to his problems. With his modest capital pouring into lawyers' pockets and no visible bottom to the slippery slope down which he slid, he readily accepted my offer for eighty acres of mixed hardwoods. It was difficult ground, and I was aware that I had paid too much: but I had sympathy with the man in his dream gone sour and I saw in him a reflection of myself. Both, in our different ways, profoundly unwordly, neither of us really understood why the world failed to adjust itself to our requirement. So I bought his timber and he gave me a site upon which to build the sawmill which had suddenly become my ambition. It seemed a natural progression for the heavy oaks and beeches which had come my way would yield firewood blocks but only as a by-product: their main use would be as squared mining timber which was much more valuable.

And then, quite suddenly and without fuss, my mother died. It is an indictment of the custom of inheritance that it is often a straight swop between the gift of security and the loss of a loved one: mine was a notable case. While I mourned my mother, dismissed her faults and interred her kindness with her bones, I was yet aware that I was now a man of independent means, and saw in a flash of honesty that my dilettante life had largely stemmed from the knowledge that I was merely marking time. In due course we assumed our substance and found that while the sums invested could no longer keep us in the style of our ancestors we had more than enough to live on. Betterburn, which

I had no intention of forsaking, would put the gilt on the gingerbread. A brave new life stretched away before us.

New lives were in vogue, for Joan was pregnant. We decided that we should stay in our rented comfortable flat until the child was born – calculations suggested it might come as an early Christmas present – and then look for a house to buy. We did not seriously consider returning to Carr Bridge and with that strange inhibition still upon us we avoided any discussion of the Bungalow's future.

I had some free and uninvested capital and it went straight into the business. My love for machinery was soon expressed in the purchase of two tractors, a diesel lorry, a heavy winch and the latest mechanical chain saw. I went to Oak in search of the components to build the sawbench. He gave me what I wanted but added one of his homilies:

'So you're going into sawmilling now, Frere?'

'Yes.'

'I was sorry to hear that your mother had died. Why don't you give up this nonsense? You'll be a wealthy man now.'

'Not very', I said. 'Things change.'

'Even so. You'll have enough to live on. I told you before, I never thought you were cut out for this game. You'll lose money over it. Ach, you're a hell of a man', he went on, seeing me so determined, 'you get too much of a kick out of life ever to be serious.' Then his expression changed: 'What's that car I saw you driving the other day? I couldn't see the make but she was a good looker.'

'An Alvis TA 14. I bought her last week.'

'That *was* a sound move.' His eyes lit up. 'I always said you had good taste in cars.'

'Thank you.'

'But if you don't mind me adding, no sense in business. Just the same the best of luck to you and keep your equipment in good order. And if you're milling, be careful. Let me see your hands.' I spread them out for his examination. 'Five on each', he remarked glumly. 'After about eighteen months some of 'em will be living on borrowed time!'

A month later the mill was built on a gravel ledge four hundred feet above Loch Ness. Protected by a tarpaulin-roofed shed, a two hundred horse-power diesel tractor drove a five-foot saw. It was the most beautiful mechanical toy. It started at the touch of a button and by cranking a handle the largest logs could be sliced and sundered. Soon I became a competent miller and could produce sawn timber to accurate measurements with very little waste. We began to get offers from local people most of whom wanted posts and wooden parts for gates but we lacked the necessary soft woods. At the same time I had heard of a firm in Aberdeen who wanted big quantities of fencing material. 'Raymond', I said, 'I wonder if the colonel would sell us that forest at the top of the hill?'

'Try him, Boss', advised Raymond.

'I certainly will.' Colonel Carson confirmed a few hours later, 'Five hundred pounds in my hand, and it's yours. And thank'ee kindly. Do you know, Frere,' he went on in a lower voice, 'they're at me again? Last week a barn was burned down and a gate left open so two of my stirks were killed on the road. This morning my water supply is dirty, not for the first time. When it happened before there were clods of earth in the well. They're doing their damndest to drive me out but by God I won't give in to 'em. Mutinous bunch of peasants. That cheque of yours will help to raise an injunction against 'em in the High Court.' His thin grey moustach bristled in his blood-suffused face and angry veins stood out. I was pleased with my purchase but depressed at his sad situation. It seemed to me that here was a case where what in the beginning had been a few hasty words, had silently escalated, fanned by mutual suspicion and the provocative exchanges of the lawyers who would be the only beneficiaries in this pointless conflict. What a breed they are! Undertakers supply a necessary service but lawyers are often pure parasites who also grow fat on other people's worms.

Throughout the winter of 1959 Betterburn prospered. We cut timber for the mines and hundreds of posts for the Aberdeen firm while the waste wood kept our firewood round intact. We had no full-time workers but a few of our faithful bus drivers helped us when their shifts allowed and in Inverness Raymond had found a number of strong schoolboys who were pleased to carry bags of wood in return for pocket money. But the great bulk of the work was shared between us and it was a brave performance for two men, a thing only made possible by our physical fitness, acceptance of long hours and the use of efficient machinery. This was a ripe moment for expansion as now I had experience behind me but my former failures had made me over cautious and I let it pass. It was an intensely enjoyable life, outdoor, active, and filled with the lusty manual skill of sawmilling. With my private means solidly behind me it seemed imprudent to search the bush for two birds when one was comfortably in my hand. In this mood of euphoria I failed to see the weakness inherent in a project which utterly depended on the unbroken participation of only two men.

Domestically we were marking time until our new child was born. Joan, indomitable even in pregnancy, took it upon herself to sort out my mother's affairs. We intended to sell the house which my mother had latterly occupied, for its situation held no charm for us and the question of where we should finally set up a family home remained undecided. Joan was as keen as ever to live in England. She enjoyed the Highland summer but she had never shared my obsession for dead grey silent rock and the stern breath of the northern winter was a punishment to her rather than an exhilarating challenge.

I was in a quandary. Had the time for such a decision coincided with one of my recessions I might have been wholehearted in wishing to try my luck elsewhere but not now. Yet though I am a selfish person, and aware of it, my wife's discontent had long affected me and I swore that as soon as our child was large enough to travel we would set out on a grand tour of the country and I would try to come to terms with what I found. I could see no reason why I should not set Raymond up as resident manager of our timber business which, if it continued to thrive, would provide me with an excuse to escape England's tame and domestic joys and get back to the mountains whenever the spirit moved me.

And then, early in December, Jane came. Unlike Dr Johnson's disparaged cat she was without doubt the finest baby in the world and not just a very fine baby. She pleased us all. Heather was now a graceful fourteen-year-old, Richard an ink-stained prep school product and with our family around us and the coffers filled to overflowing we settled down to enjoy a good Christmas.

Jane was five months old when we started our journey in search of pastures new. In the Spring sunlight, each with our private emotions, Joan and I dropped down through the great Redesdale forest into the England that was native to us both. I had left Raymond and our bus drivers to work the mill.

Our wanderings took us to the far corners of the kingdom. We stayed with cousins in Norfolk and looked at many houses there but none was right for us. We exchanged the flintstone heaths and vanished meres of my childhood for the rolling downs and leafy lanes where Joan had spent hers. We read through the advertisements in *Country Life* and followed glossy photographic images to sober reality in the powerful hood-down Alvis in the burning Summer weather. At last after much searching and many disappointments we returned to our cousins. In our absence they had been busy on our behalf and had found something which we had missed. It was what Joan wanted, and I had to admit that it had much to recommend it. It was a pretty house, alone though not remote, and it stood on the edge of a wide common through which ran that same River Waveney whose upper reaches my father had formerly owned. It would have been nice to have exclaimed: 'Here I am, home at last!' but the sentiment would have rung as off-tune as a cracked bell. My home, the place which suited every facet of my nature, was beyond the Highland line and the prospect of idle rustication in this pleasant but unexciting country filled me with depression.

The next morning we met the owners to discuss the price: it was within our means. Joan was overjoyed and the two elder children had caught on to her mood. How I wished I might have shared their jubilation! I put as brave a face as possible on it and simulated an interest in the place which I did not feel. I owed it to Joan to accept my sacrifice as for a decade she had accepted hers, but it was not going to be easy. In what way could I possibly occupy my time? Building work for which I had acquired a considerable taste at the Bungalow would not exist for the new house was drearily complete and immaculate. Already there had been a hint of an unending social round which would surely erode my substance, my health and finally my individuality. A conventional life lay ahead as flat and lacking in outstanding feature as the East Anglian landscape for here, in this land of my fathers, there were many things which one 'did not do'. Worst of all I was beginning to have the gravest doubts as to whether Betterburn would go on without me: to run such a venture successfully was much to ask of a seventeen-year-old boy. If only Bob had been available it might have been a different matter. The two of them would have managed it admirably but Bob had returned to Carr Bridge and married a widow: he had gone beyond recall. Without my business in the North I would neither have the means nor the inducement (excuse might be the better word) to get back to my mountains.

In fact I need not have worried. A twist of fate confirmed me in my selfish course. My lawyers had found and made much of a small complication in my father's will and acted to overcome it with the sloth of snails. While they were engaged in ponderous exchanges the sellers of the Norfolk house grew weary, then urgent and the house was sold to others while we waited. It nearly broke Joan's heart.

We returned to our rented flat in the North but that

situation had now become a temporary one for the house had come on the market. We were given first refusal but we turned it down. It was too rambling and Victorian for Joan; too much in need of major repair and too close to Inverness for either of us. But we had to move and quite by chance we heard of a country house near the village of Drumna-drochit. It had not been publicly advertised and we had admired it when passing by, not knowing that it was within our reach. Long, low and dignified, and some of it of antique date, my wife saw a challenge in its restoration. Previous owners had dressed it up cheaply in the tawdry trappings of the present day, good mutton passing for poor lamb. Indignant at such insulting treatment, Joan took the stately building to her heart; we bought it, and we live there still.

In my absence Raymond had been a good steward. He had cut down hundreds of trees and driven their sections to the mill for machining. Trade was still good but the demands of our new house were great: my own income and the yield from Betterburn could hardly keep pace. Soon I must purchase more standing timber. We worked these days under anxious pressure, my carefree pleasure in the job transformed by sober necessity. But we knew what we could do because we had done it already. I was under contract to provide several loads of square chocks for a Scottish pit but there was a strict time limit on the arrangement. We toiled unceasingly through the dying days of autumn until we were all but deafened by the scream of the saws and blinded by their dust. At last we both admitted to being tired. Two loads were ready, a third was building up. A contractor, going south with empty vehicles, had agreed to uplift the lot on cheap terms if we could have it ready for him in a week's time. Fearing we should not meet the deadline I fitted a second saw to the mill so that Raymond might work beside me, squaring the ends of the sawn blocks. The resulting uproar was so tremendous that it made concentration difficult, the working area so cramped that we got in each other's way. A fool could have seen that we were all set for a mishap.

It came on a wet October morning. We had been milling for no longer than an hour but already we were tense and irritable. The timber was dry and tight grained: it gripped the spinning blades, causing them to warp with the heat of friction. The logs shook violently on the greasy bench. I was struggling to engage one with my blade when I heard Raymond shout in a high agonised voice. I turned to him: he stood a little way back from the bench, bent forward with his left hand clasping his right wrist, and on his dead white face was a look of shocked disbelief. As though to convince himself he slowly removed his hand and frowningly observed the mangled thing beneath it: 'Good God, Boss', he said, almost conversationally, 'that's a mess, isn't it?' As I moved to his aid a jet of his blood sprayed my face with the force of a stirrup-pump.

With my torn-up shirt I garrotted the arm at the elbow. The pumping slowed to a welling up but I could see his forearm was in ruins. His grip had slipped from the chock and his extended hand had gone right into the blade. Dazed by the impact he had stumbled forward and to protect his chest had used his bent forearm: the saw had ripped open the length of it. The shredded flesh revealed a tangle of cut arteries and snipped white ligaments. But the hand looked even worse, if such a thing were possible, for the bones at the base of the thumb were smashed.

He was barely conscious when they helped him from my car at an Inverness hospital and I had to strain my ears to hear his words of apology: 'Sorry, Boss, it was careless of me. Just as we were trying to make up that load. I'm afraid I'll not be able to come back for a week or two.' I told him not to worry even as I wondered how I came to deserve such loyalty. I didn't expect that he'd ever be back or that he'd regain the use of that hand. In fact I imagined he'd be lucky if they didn't cut it off.

But thanks to fine surgery it stayed with him. The early prognosis was relatively good. His surgeon told me on the telephone that it might take months to regain even a measure of movement in the joint but he would finally be left with only small disability. I thanked God for that and wondered why those who served me best always paid so dearly for that doubtful privilege. Oak had certainly been right: 'You're a man who attracts trouble.' There seemed to be no end to my ability to provoke the Furies.

Yet as a final irony it was not Raymond's massive injury but a tiny splinter in my own hand which liquidated Better- burn. This fateful sliver had entered my palm before his accident: within a few days it became septic. With difficulty I put off the contractor and his lorries while I toiled alone and in great pain to complete the milling of the third load. Before it was finished my palm was swollen like a tight, crimson balloon and the poison brought lassitude and a strong nausea. It also affected my reason in that I became obsessed with the thought that I must not seek medical attention until I had carried out my self-appointed task.

Richard spent the last day with me. He was home for his half-term holiday and had pestered Joan until she agreed to let him accompany me. She made me promise to keep him away from the machinery and do nothing other than stack the cut chocks and keep me in cups of tea. This was always made in an old black kettle which sat, tinker fashion, on a pile of burning logs. By afternoon he had made up his mind that these simple activities were preferable to the study of French and English and he suggested that he leave school and become a timber merchant like myself. Extreme pain makes hearty laughter difficult but I managed a wry grimace and a firm shake of the head: 'Don't say that, my boy. Not in my company. It might happen to you.'

'But I'd like it, Daddy, really!'

'Mummy and I want you to go to Sandhurst for the Army.'

'I don't think I need to be killed in peacetime.'

'We don't want you to be killed at all, but it's an honour- able profession and in keeping with our ancient name. Do you know, sometimes I wonder why I'm doing this sort of thing? It's like a nightmare.'

'You've done lots of things in your time, haven't you, Daddy?'

'Yes, too damn many, if you'll pardon my French, and they've all been wrong. At moments like this one sees the light.'

'Can we go for a climb during my half-term?'

'Now you're talking. But I must go to the doctor and have my hand lanced first, and I can't do that until this load is finished. Then we'll go for a climb. But wait a moment –'

'Yes, Daddy?'

'I believe a spell of walking might make me feel better. Let's take the afternoon off and climb up to that crag which you can see on the skyline. I've never taken you there before, but it's a place I used to know well as a boy. We'll make up that load this evening: it's just about done anway.'

'That'd be super fun. Shall I pour water on the fire before we go?'

'No, don't bother, it's quite safe. Leave the kettle to keep warm near it.'

I switched off the tractor engine and an afternoon calm settled on the mill site. Then we clambered slowly over steep scree and waded through heather into the birch beyond Colonel Carson's land. It was a soft October day with a growing west wind beginning to rustle the drying, browning leaves. We climbed higher, enjoying the view. The air was unusually clear. The low Monadhliath mountains stood like cardboard cuttings beyond the valley of the Nairn River where every house was perfect in its tiny detail. My arm ached less as the exercise took blood to my legs but I was still oddly light headed and my cheeks were flushed as though by fever. I had a great wish to talk and to go on talking.

Before long we came to a harsh slit in the red sandstone of the hill. 'We'll work our way round to those trees', I said, 'on the very edge of the gully. It's a most dramatic place. As boys we used to come up to it from below which was a suicidal thing to do. The rock is as soft as cake. But somehow nothing ever happened to us.'

When we reached the trees I said: 'This is it then. If you take my hand you can peep down the precipice. Good, isn't it? And listen to the wind in these pine trees. And smell them. How sounds and smell act on the memory! I remember a particular day when I came here once, alone. It must have been twenty-five years ago. Maybe more. But it sticks out because it contained a moment when I suddenly realised what a lucky boy I was. Your grandparents, although it cost them their peace of mind, never stopped me adventuring. Most of the time I took it for granted. Then all at once I found myself rejoicing in my wonderful good fortune in being free to do the thing I liked best. And what a future lay ahead. I was going to climb every big mountain in the world – well it hasn't worked out like that. Do you want some chocolate?'

'Thank you, Daddy. Daddy what's that funny smell?'

'I've just been telling you, it's from the pines. And it's not a funny smell, it's a beautiful one. Sometimes I think I'm talking to –'

'No', he interrupted, 'not that one. It's like well, rubber or something. It's coming from the direction of the mill and I think we ought to go down. Look at all the smoke.'

We ran back the way we had come. While we were still in the birches there was a hollow boom and I could see a small black mushroom cloud through the leaves. It was perfectly obvious that the tank of the tractor, newly filled, had just blown up. Richard, running by my side, asked nervously: 'Oh Daddy, what's that?'

'Nemesis', I replied, to his great bewilderment.

The next morning I went to the doctor and had about a pint of pus let out of my hand. The relief gave me the strength to drive out to the ruins. As I was poking about in them who should turn up but John Oak. Of all the men in the world he was the last one I wanted to see then.

'This is bad work, Frere,' he said. 'How did it happen?'

I shrugged my shoulders defensively. 'I suppose it was the small fire on which we boiled the kettle. It must have spread along the sawdust and caught waste oil under the tractor tank.'

'But where were you? Couldn't you have stopped it?'

'There was no one here. My son and I had gone climbing', I answered, aware of how ridiculous it sounded.

'Where was your man?'

'In hospital. He put his arm in the saw yesterday.' I was heartily sick of his questions.

He nodded: it was obviously no surprise to him. 'Yes, I suppose. What shall you do now? There isn't much left here.' That was true. The tractor was a blackened, broken wreck, tyres burnt away and a great hole had been blown in its tank. The bench had gone and the supports of the vanished awning were short charred stumps. It had rained in the night: the steel of the circular saws, warped and softened, was already red with rust.

'You were insured, of course', he said flatly.

'Do you take me for a normal person?' I asked; 'Not a hope. You must know me well enough to realise I can never anticipate mishaps.'

'It's a pity', he said, 'for I was about to congratulate you. These chocks look like the work of a professional miller. You've arranged haulage I suppose?'

'Yes. I found a contractor with three empty lorries and no work this week. He was delighted to do it cheap.'

'You *are* learning. No longer wet behind the ears when it comes to bargaining. God, but you were hopeless to start with. That stuff you bought from me! I remember the day you came into my office when you were after the Canadian Ford. You said you'd give me fifty quid for it before I could open my mouth. It was worth twenty-five and I'd have settled for forty. Well, I should have been so stupid – but, anyway, you have a good few hundred pounds of timber on this bank.'

'It's my gratuity then, my golden handshake with myself. I'm packing in.'

'Believe it or not, I'm sorry to hear you say so. Does that surprise you? You've learnt a trade the hard way and you've learnt it well, and that's a thing I have a rare fancy for. Going to write another book?'

'Oh that! Perhaps I will. But just now I've enough to do. We're doing a lot of work on our new house at Drumnadrochit.'

'Modernising it?'

'You don't know my wife! No, restoring it to its proper period.'

'I see. And what about the place at Carr Bridge? You won't leave that to fall down, I hope. Property up there will soon get valuable.'

'I'm afraid it's pretty derelict by now. The winters up there play the devil with empty houses. But we intend to go and see quite soon. It may not be as bad as we think. By the way, will you come to a house warming at Drumnadrochit next week? My wife was going to phone you to give you a firm date nearer the time. But it'll be Friday week.'

'Thank her, I'll be fair chuffed to come', he said warmly, his devils' eyebrows slanting, 'and it puts me in mind of that big open air party which I gate-crashed at Moy! As long as I live I sha'n't ever forget coming over that bank and seeing all those drunks lying about in the middle of my ruined timber. I said to myself then, I know that bugger Frere's mad.' He began to laugh uproariously at the thought of it and I latched on to his mood. While we were still chuckling together three big lorries came rumbling up the hill to pick up my timber.

16 ❧ A Ticket Cancelled

I had been a gentleman of leisure for six months when, in the early Spring of 1961, we plucked up the courage to raise old ghosts and see what total neglect and six Carr Bridge winters had done to the Bungalow. It had recently occurred to us that unless it was actually devastated by frost, wind and damp so as to make economic repair impossible it might yet become an investment. Thanks to the big development in neighbouring Speyside and the presence of a ski school in the Wilshins' former guesthouse at Struan there was now a winter as well as a summer season and we saw no reason why some of the area's new-found wealth might not rub off on us. It could be an unexpected justification and reward for the years of hard work and turn our many disappointments into a belated success.

We drove there on a typical April day, the wind and the rain were flying and the Slochd summit was grey with a lamb storm's melted snow. As we came down the last hill into the village, between the tiny forest of new trees which Bob and I had helped to plant, I could see the great ice palaces of Cairngorm's northern corries flashing in the scurrying bursts of sun. I thought of Peter Randall with mixed feelings and wondered what had become of him.

The Station Road was much as we remembered it, though smaller and shorter – an odd trick of time's passage. 'I'd like to have a pound', I said to Joan, 'for every time we walked or motorcycled up here.' She smiled: 'In my case, bicycled. As a matter of fact I used to quite enjoy it, pushing away with the groceries in my basket.' Now we could safely recall both the good things and the bad, the good tended to predominate. And suddenly, there was the best of them. 'Stop!' she cried, 'it's Bob. I know it is!' I followed her pointing finger to where a black tammy was just visible above a neatly clipped hedge. 'It will be', I answered, equally excited 'that's Mrs McTurk's garden. He's been digging it for years! This is going to make our day. Come on, let's give him a surprise.' We left the car a few yards up the road and crept back, crouching beneath the hedge. He had his back to us as he drove his spade industriously into the half-frozen soil. 'Shush!' said Joan as I was about to shout 'Bob', and then she said to him: 'Excuse me, do you think you could direct us to the Bungalow?'

He spun round; the spade fell from his hand. 'Holy Old Smoke!' he cried out to our great delight. 'Where did youse folks spring from?' He looked exactly the same as when we had seen him first. We explained the reason for our presence. 'Come on', I said, 'they're open. We've so much to tell you. Let's do it over some drams.'

A bit later I ended our recent history with: 'And so we thought we'd have a look at the old place. If it isn't too bad we might be able to let it to the tourists. And maybe you could see them in and out for us?'

Bob said 'Oh' and looked at the floor.

'It's still there, isn't it?' joked Joan.

'Yes it is that,' he answered slowly, 'but it's no' great. Ye see, I reckon ye should have told the copper to keep an eye on it. Soon as I came back here I went to look and well – some bad local loons had made a right mess of it. Times later I caught one of the little beggars at it and scalped the living daylights out of him, but it wasn'a any good.'

'Let's all go up now.'

'I'll no come', he said firmly, 'I couldn'a be with you when you see how it is. Not after all the work youse young people put into it. I reckon it would just about break my heart. The nice 'uns around here still talk about it, how you built the house together and the schemes you tried –'

Joan said: 'But Bob, remember how you helped us. Without your support I don't think we could have carried on.'

'I should have been here', he said illogically, 'it's as though I've let you down.'

So we left him and slowly drove up the road, halted the

car and walked up the overgrown path. What the winters
had done was no surprise. The elements had acted in
accordance with their natures and had inflicted predictable
wounds. The walls were stained yellow with damp, the
paint on the front door was flaked while the foundations
had stirred in the sand leaving cracks in the structure into
which the frost had driven its icy wedge. The concrete
surfaces were crazed with cracks. None of this was worse
than we expected and no less than we deserved for having
left the house so long untended. But what had happened
inside we had *not* deserved and the impact of it was so sharp
that I saw Joan tremble and I let out an involuntary shout:
'There have been madmen here!'

The interior of the little house, once our home, where
every act of making had been done with some love and care
had been totally vandalised. Nothing that could be broken
remained intact. The glass was gone from the windows, the
panels from the doors. As we saw the full extent of this
mindless destruction a great rage rose in me: had I had the
ill doers within my hands I would have punished them to
the danger of their lives. For it was a part of our lives that
they had killed in a crime that lacked even the mitigation of
personal gain.

In a stunned and bitter silence we went through the
house. Where the new partitions had been we moved as
ghosts, passing easily through vanished walls. They had
been torn down, splintered and thrown through open window frames. On the grass outside there was a grey patch of
wet ash with a few rusty nails and brackets showing. Here
there had been, perhaps, a bonfire in the honour of that
terrorist Guy Fawkes: but he, at least, had conceived his
destructive plan as a national duty. The hot water cylinder
had gone, the pipes had been torn from the walls, electric
wiring hung down from the ceiling like overgrown cobwebs.
The kitchen sink, wash basin and lavatory pan had been
cracked like eggs. The Rayburn, too solid to shatter, had
escaped with starred enamel and the loss of its oven door. A
book, or books, had been burned within it.

We had locked the guardsvan against intrusion but my abandoned wrecking bar had provided a key to it. As though inflamed by this attempt at security the vandals had worked with renewed fury. The few possessions we had stored there had been systematically violated. Chairs were smashed, a child's bed ripped open and the old radiogram which had once played Sibelius and his peers with such gusto had been kicked in and eviscerated. Its innards lay everywhere, scattered around as though by the pluck of vultures' beaks. But vultures can be vindicated for they use entrails for food.

'I can't understand it', said Joan, in a sad daze, 'nothing has been *stolen*. This has been done for fun. It's as though they hated us.' And this was true for if, as we must assume, big, vicious children, in their state of original sin, had been the culprits where were the parents, who must have known us or known of us, when these shameful things were being done? And if they knew why had they not cared enough to ensure a halt?

We did not linger, the scene lay upon our spirits like a pall. There was no prospect for the place but demolition and the subsequent sale of the site. It set a seal of dreary futility upon the record of the time spent under this roof but to me it was also a chilling indictment of an unforeseeing selfish, obsession-ridden state of mind which had governed these years and those which had followed them. It was one of those moments of self-realisation and I was moved to remark with some sincerity: 'I'm very sorry. It was a waste of a lot of your life.'

She nodded: it could hardly be denied. 'It was the winters', she said, 'the long dreary winters and waiting for a spring that never came. But I'm still alive, the children grew up well and you followed your star. Or stars. And I wouldn't have missed the chance of meeting Bob and Mrs Leslie and the others who helped to make it bearable.' She looked around her sadly. 'Poor little house – it never really had a chance, did it? All our plans, fine plans, and now look at it. Well, we've done with it now and the years are in the dustbin. It's a chapter ended but there is still most of the book to come.'

'Yes', I said, 'that's true. It's nice of you to take it so well, just the same. Perhaps in the fullness of time nostalgia will pick out something to remember with pleasure. Come on, let's go home.'

We went out into a brisk April shower. The sleet stung our faces as we went down the overgrown steps which we had built together. I was still mumbling self-indulgent apologies as I started the car. Joan said, 'Oh do shut up! You're making a meal of it, as usual. There isn't any more to say. I married you, didn't I? But if you must, let Heather have the last word.

'Heather?'

'Yes. Do you remember what an easy-going child she was? But when she'd been naughty, which wasn't often, and had made a mistake which couldn't be put right, she'd often say: "So's all about it". Quite final, that was.'

'So's all about it', I echoed, feeling absolved, as we drove away in a patch of scurrying sunshine.

SELECTED NON-FICTION TITLES
AVAILABLE FROM CORGI BOOKS

WHILE EVERY EFFORT IS MADE TO KEEP PRICES LOW, IT IS SOME-
TIMES NECESSARY TO INCREASE PRICES AT SHORT NOTICE. CORGI
BOOKS RESERVE THE RIGHT TO SHOW NEW RETAIL PRICES ON
COVERS WHICH MAY DIFFER FROM THOSE PREVIOUSLY ADVERTISED
IN THE TEXT OR ELSEWHERE.

THE PRICES SHOWN BELOW WERE CORRECT AT THE TIME OF GOING
TO PRESS (APRIL '85).

*All these books are available at your book shop or newsagent, or can be ordered
direct from the publisher. Just tick the titles you want and fill in the form below.*

CORGI BOOKS, Cash Sales Department, P.O. Box 11, Falmouth, Cornwall.

Please send cheque or postal order, no currency.

Please allow cost of book(s) plus the following for postage and packing:

U.K. Customers—Allow 55p for the first book, 22p for the second book and 14p for
each additional book ordered, to a maximum charge of £1.75.

B.F.P.O. and Eire—Allow 55p for the first book, 22p for the second book plus 14p
per copy for the next seven books, thereafter 8p per book.

Overseas Customers—Allow £1.00 for the first book and 25p per copy for each
additional book.

NAME (Block Letters) ....

ADDRESS ....

....